THE

CAMPAIGNS OF HANNIBAL

THE

CAMPAIGNS OF HANNIBAL

ARRANGED AND CRITICALLY CONSIDERED

P ATRICK L EONARD M AC D OUGALL

WESTHOLME

Yardley

Originally published in 1858 by Longman, Brown, Green, Longmans, &
Roberts

This edition copyright © 2007 Westholme Publishing

Westholme Publishing, LLC
Eight Harvey Avenue
Yardley, Pennsylvania 19067
Visit our Web site at www.westholmepublishing.com

First Edition: October 2007
10 9 8 7 6 5 4 3 2 1

ISBN: 978-1-59416-056-1
ISBN 10: 1-59416-056-2

Printed in

PUBLISHER'S NOTE.

———

Throughout this history references are made to "observations." These follow each chapter. In addition, the author refers on occasion to his *The Theory of War* (1858). For the convenience of the reader, these references have been added following the last chapter. A general index has also been compiled and included at the end of the book.

MAP

TO ILLUSTRATE THE

CAMPAIGNS OF HANNIBAL

in

ITALY.

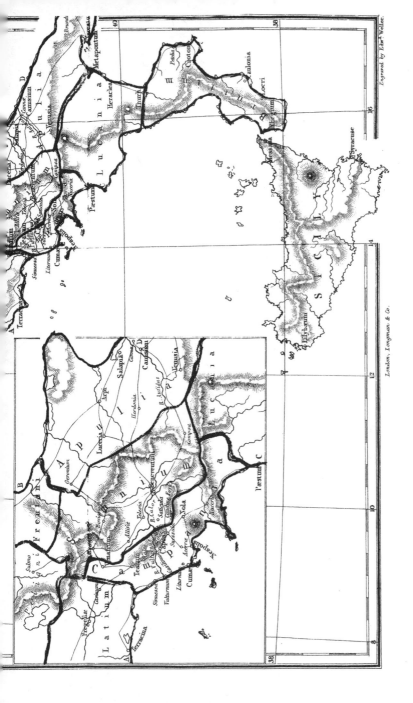

Engraved by Edwd. Weller.

London, Longman. & Co.

PREFACE.

THE following Narrative of the Campaigns of Hannibal has been carefully compiled from the different and, in many cases, differing accounts of the best ancient and modern historians and essayists, including Livy, Polybius, Sir Walter Raleigh, Niebuhr, Arnold, Guiscard, and Vaudancourt.

I have confined myself to the operations in which Hannibal was personally engaged, merely alluding to the contemporaneous events, military and political, in Africa, Spain, and Sicily, and pointing out the effect which they exercised on the contest in Italy, and on the final evacuation of that peninsula by Hannibal.

I have endeavoured to avoid fatiguing the reader with useless details, and to present only to his notice the more salient points, which will enable him to form some conception of the vast genius of the great Carthaginian, and to draw the clearest military lessons therefrom.

The events of Hannibal's career convey so useful a lesson to the military student, that all officers should be intimately acquainted with them. But comparatively few are so. Many have heard of the Trebbia, of Thrasymene, and Cannæ; — are aware that Fabius was called " Cunctator," and have a general impression that he was rather a slow coach; — but of the real greatness of Hannibal and of the Roman commanders opposed to him, as well as of the gigantic difficulties he successfully overcame, their knowledge is for the most part very imperfect.

The subject is one of the greatest interest, and if it is not found to be so in the following pages it is the writer's blame.

At the end of each campaign will be found critical remarks on its most salient points; and my object has been to arrange the narrative in that way that shall be the easiest and most instructive to the military student.

Royal Military College, Sandhurst:
Feb. 1, 1858.

CONTENTS.

	Page
INTRODUCTORY ACCOUNT OF THE ORGANISATION OF THE	
ROMAN AND GREEK ARMIES	1
ROMAN ORGANISATION	1
Light Infantry	1
Heavy Infantry	2
Cavalry	2
Staff Officers	6
Chief of the Staff.—Civil Departments . .	7
Artillery	8
Manœuvres	8
Marches	9
Encampments	9
GREEK ORGANISATION	10
Infantry, Light and Heavy	11
The Phalanx	11
Infantry Formation	12
Cavalry Formation	12
INTRODUCTORY CHAPTER	15
CHAP. I.—March into Italy and First Campaign . .	24
Battle of the Trebbia	40
Observations	43

	Page
Chap. II. — Second Campaign	53
Battle of Thrasymene	59
Observations	76
Chap. III. — Third Campaign	85
Battle of Cannæ	87
Observations	98
Chap. IV. — Fourth Campaign	107
Fifth Campaign	114
Observations	122
Chap. V. — Sixth Campaign	128
Seventh Campaign	132
Eighth Campaign	135
Observations	144
Chap. VI. — Ninth Campaign	150
Tenth Campaign	156
Eleventh Campaign	158
Twelfth Campaign	162
Thirteenth Campaign	166
Nero's famous March	170
Battle of the Metaurus	172
Observations	175
Concluding Chapter	181
Battle of the Zama	186
Observations	191

THE CAMPAIGNS OF HANNIBAL.

INTRODUCTORY ACCOUNT

OF THE ORGANISATION OF THE ROMAN AND GREEK ARMIES.

THE Roman army was divided into legions, each legion answering to our division; and was supposed to be complete within itself.

The infantry was divided into Light and Heavy armed.

Light Infantry.

The Light-armed infantry — called, until the Siege of Capua, *Rorarii*, afterwards *Velites* — carried the short cut-and-thrust Roman sword twenty and a half inches long, a small round shield, and seven light darts, each four feet long with a sharp iron point.

Heavy Infantry.

The Heavy-armed infantry was composed of three classes: *Hastati, Principes,* and *Triarii.*

The *Hastati* formed the first of the three lines in which the legionary heavy infantry was drawn up.

The *Principes* formed the second line.

The *Hastati* and *Principes* were armed as follows:— Each soldier wore a breastplate or coat of mail, brazen greaves, and a brazen helmet with a lofty crest of scarlet or black feathers, and carried a large oblong shield. His offensive weapons were the short cut-and-thrust sword worn on the right thigh, and in his hand, besides a lighter javelin, he grasped the formidable pilum. This weapon was a ponderous javelin, nearly eight feet long, having a shaft of four feet and an iron head of nearly equal length; and although very inferior to the modern musket, since it was capable of only one discharge, yet when it was launched by a strong and practised hand at the distance of ten or twelve paces, there was not any shield or breastplate that could withstand its shock.

The *Triarii* formed the third line. They consisted of veteran soldiers who carried the same equipment as the *Principes* and *Hastati* excepting that in place of the pilum and javelin they were armed with pikes about eleven feet in length.

Cavalry.

A small body of Cavalry formed a component part of each legion. The Cavalry soldier was armed originally in the same manner as the *Rorarii* or Light infantry; but afterwards the Greek equipment was adopted and the trooper was armed with a helmet, cuirass, buckler, and greaves; and for offensive weapons with a spear and sabre.

The strength of the legion varied at different periods, and with it the strength of the different lines, although their proportion to each other remained the same.

During the Second Punic war the infantry of the legion was fixed at 5000 men.

The	first	line,	*Hastati*,	numbered	. .	1600
"	second	"	*Principes*	"	. .	1600
"	third	"	*Triarii*	"	. .	600

Total heavy infantry	3800
Light infantry	1200
Total infantry . . .	5000

Each line was subdivided into ten maniples, each maniple again into two centuries.

A maniple of *Hastati* or *Principes* consisted therefore of 160 men, formed in ten ranks of sixteen files each.

A maniple of *Triarii*, of sixty men, formed in five ranks of twelve files each.

The files as well as the ranks stood three feet apart, that is to say, each file occupied three feet of front as well as three feet in depth.

The centuries were commanded by officers called Centurions. But the Roman infantry unit was the *maniple*, which consisted of two centuries in line ; and was commanded by the senior of the two Centurions.

During the second Punic war the heavy Roman infantry was usually formed in three lines, at distances apart of about 100 yards.

The ten maniples of which each line was composed had intervals between them equal to the front of a maniple ; and instead of covering those of the line in front of them, the maniples of the second and third lines covered the intervals.

This open order was convenient for marching, but was unsuitable for fighting any but an enemy who adopted the same formation. When the legion was opposed to troops ranged in close order, it became necessary to conform to that order; and this was effected by the simple advance of the maniples of the second line to fill the intervals of the first.

The open order was, moreover, especially dangerous where the enemy had a superior cavalry, as the relative nature of the two arms at the time we refer to enabled cavalry to approach, with impunity, within fifteen yards of infantry ; and to dash at any weak point with great effect.

The battle was invariably commenced by the light troops who, formed in four or five ranks, skirmished in front of the legion ; but when the time came to charge they passed through the intervals of the heavy infantry, and formed up in the intervals between the maniples of *Triarii*.

Then, advancing to the charge, the men of the first line discharged first their javelins at an approaching enemy; afterwards when within twelve paces, their *pila;* after which they drew their swords for the hand-to-hand contest.

Cavalry.

The Cavalry of the legion was fixed at 320 men and horses, divided into ten troops, each troop being formed in four ranks of eight files. Three officers called Decurions were attached to each troop, which was commanded by the senior Decurion.

Every Roman legion had attached to it in the field a legion of Italian allies, of precisely the same strength and organisation as above stated, excepting that the legionary *allied* horse numbered 600 instead of 300. Therefore, for the strength of every legion of the Roman army employed in the field, we may compute 10,000 infantry and 900 cavalry.

The front occupied by two such combined legions, or by *one legion,* under which term they are invariably comprised by the historians of the period, is thus calculated : —

20 Legionary maniples of 16 files, each file occupying one
    yard, and with intervals equal to the front of a maniple, viz.:
    $20 \times 16 \times 2 =$.   .   .   . 640 yards
900 cavalry in 4 ranks of 225 files, each file occupying 1 yard = 225

                                                           ————
                                                            865
                     Or about half a mile.

At a later period the formation by maniples was replaced by that of cohorts.

One cohort consisted of one maniple of each of the three lines, either covering each other or having the maniples of the *Hastati* and *Principes* in the same line, and the maniple of the *Triarii* in rare. This arrangement of cohorts superseded that of three lines. Each cohort formed one compact body drawn up in ten ranks.

In the first formation just given, the *Hastati* occupied the four first ranks, the *Principes* the four next; and the *Triarii* the two last. In the second formation the *Principes* and *Hastati*, side by side, occupied the eight first ranks; the *Triarii* the two last as before.

The legion was thus composed of ten cohorts, which were disposed in two or three lines as most convenient.

The Roman Generals, under the title of consuls or prætors, were elected yearly by the people. This system was doubtless adopted from a fear lest a successful General, left too long in command, might gain sufficient influence over his troops to enable him to seize on supreme authority. A yearly change of Commanders, however, if rigidly enforced, would render success impossible in a protracted war, and in times of emergency it was found necessary to continue the same generals in command, either under the title of proconsul or proprætor, or to re-elect them to their offices for another year. The military authority of the Consuls was coequal and supreme. A Consular army usually consisted of two legions numbering 20,000 infantry, and 1800 cavalry; the army of a prætor might consist of one or two legions, according to circumstances.

Staff Officers.

Military tribunes were legionary officers, whose functions were more those of superior Staff Officers than to exercise any distinct command; they had the general superintendence of the working of all the different departments of the army.

Under them subordinate Staff Officers were employed, under the names of *Anti-mensores* and *Anti-censores* whose business was to furnish correct intelligence regarding all points connected with the marches of the army, such as state of the roads, rivers, resources of country, halting places, &c.; and to mark out the general camping ground. *Mensores* and *Censores,* charged with the details of the actual camp, its measurement, and construction, &c.

Exploratores and *Sulcatores,* whose sole duty was to reconnoitre the enemy and to furnish every possible information regarding him.

Chief of the Staff.—Civil Department.

Every Roman army had attached to it an officer who, under the name of Quæstor or Prefect, performed the duties of a Chief of the Staff, and was next in authority to the Commander. He had the particular control as well of the military as of the Civil departments, in which last were comprised those of the Paymaster and Commissary-General, and what we should call the Medical Service.

The Commissariat arrangements were very elaborate; it is unnecessary to enter into them; but connected with the medical service it is interesting to notice the existence of a body of men whose duties were analogous to those of the French " Infirmiers," and of our own

Military Train on a field of battle. The duty of these men, who were called "depotates" and were selected for their activity and courage, was to carry off the wounded during a battle. Posted in small companies of ten together along the rear of the first line, they were provided with horses carrying double panniers (a rude sort of "cacolet") for the conveyance of the wounded who were unable to walk; and their devotion was stimulated by a reward in money for every wounded man they saved.

A body of military artificers was attached to each legion, who were employed in the manufacture of tools and in the construction of military machines.

Artillery.

During the second Punic war we do not read of any field artillery, but at a later period each maniple had attached to it a *balista*, mounted on a car drawn by mules and served by eleven men of the maniple. The balistæ propelled bolts or darts with great force, and were placed in battery on the field. Besides these a more powerful engine, called a catapult, was attached to each Cohort; it was employed rather in defending the approaches to the camp, than on the field of battle.

Manœuvres.

In adverting to the manœuvres of the legion it is only necessary to remark that the formations of line, column, and echellon were in common use.

In modern times artillery is the arm preponderance

in which has told most in favour of the army possessing it. But at the period of the second Punic war, cavalry unquestionably exercised the most important effect on the issue of an engagement, and it will be found that in almost every pitched battle fought during this period the contest was decided by the cavalry.

Marches.

The length of a legionary soldier's daily march was from twenty to twenty-five miles, and it must be remembered that he carried armour.

An advanced and rear guard of light cavalry and infantry preceded and closed the march, which was always conducted on as wide a front as possible, to enable the line of battle to be formed with the least possible delay.

Encampments.

Roman Generals, when within reach of an enemy, invariably fortified their camps. The small range of ancient artillery, about 400 yards, permitted hostile armies to encamp at little more than that distance from each other. In a temporary camp, where the army would not remain more than one or two nights, it was enough to dig a trench sufficient to form a parapet six inches thick at the top, and three feet high. In permanent camps the ditch was usually about nine feet deep, and from nine to seventeen feet wide ; the parapet ten feet high, and ten or twelve feet thick, raised on a foundation of trunks of trees, and built up with branches and brushwood. *Abattis* were frequently constructed beyond the ditch, and a flanking defence for the straight sides of the camp was obtained by throwing out a circular sort of bastion in the centre of each side, as well as at the angles.

It is remarkable that during the second Punic war we do not read of the employment of field artillery by either party, although Alexander the Great used balistæ at the battle of the Granicus 100 years before.

The organisation of the Greek armies, on which that of the Carthaginians was based, was as follows:—

The simple or single phalanx consisted of—

Heavy infantry numbering	4096 men
Light infantry	2048
Total infantry of the Phalanx . .	6144

The cavalry of the phalanx consisted of two regiments, or hipparcheis, of 512 horses each.

The heavy infantry was of two kinds,—

1st. The *Hoplites*, armed with a short sword; the formidable pike or *Sarissa*, twenty-four feet long; a helmet, cuirass, greaves, and a small round shield.

2nd. The *Peltastes*, who carried a shorter pike, a light coat of mail, a smaller buckler, and lighter armour generally than the hoplites.

The light infantry soldier, called the *psiles*, wore no defensive armour beyond a quilted cap and tunic; and his offensive weapons were the bow and arrow, light darts, and the sling.

The cavalry was likewise divided into light and heavy. Alexander the Great formed a body of cavalry similar to the original dragoons, who fought equally on foot or horseback.

The heavy cavalry wore coats of mail, helmets, and brazen greaves, — their offensive weapons were a short thrusting pike and a sword.

The light cavalry carried lances about sixteen feet long, and were chiefly employed in outpost duty.

The phalangite heavy infantry of 4096 men was divided into eight battalions, or pentekosiarchys, of 512 men each, and descending the scale we arrive at the successive subdivisions of the demi-battalion, or *syntagma*, of 256 men; and the *lochos*, of 16 men.

The *lochos*, the basis of the phalangite formation, was simply one file extending from front to rear of the phalanx, which was drawn up in sixteen ranks.

The *syntagma* was the lochos squared; that is to say, it consisted of sixteen files as well as sixteen ranks, and was the smallest body which could conveniently act independently, because a smaller body would have more ranks than files, and in marching to a flank it would move on a wider front than when advancing to its proper front. The *syntagma* is the natural unit of the Greek military organisation.

The unit of light infantry was the *hécatontarchy*, or company, of 128 men; the light infantry of the phalanx (2048 men) was drawn up in eight ranks only, in place of sixteen, and its successive subdivisions corresponded to those of the phalangite heavy infantry, but were only half the strength of the latter. The light troops were sometimes drawn up behind the phalanx, whence it shot darts or arrows over the heads of that body; sometimes on the flanks, and sometimes incorporated in the phalanx itself.

The formation of the phalangite heavy infantry was by double battalions, or chiliarchys, numbering 1024 men each, drawn up in line with intervals of 10 paces.

These bodies were commanded by officers called Chiliarchs, the battalions by Pentecosiarchs, and each further subdivision by its appropriate subordinate officer.

This formation by double battalions in line, was that always practised by Hannibal during the second Punic war.

Cavalry Formation.

The formation of the cavalry was occasionally in the figure of a rhombus, or of a wedge; but the prevailing order was in eight ranks. The cavalry unit was the square of eight files, or sixty-four men, which may be regarded as a troop. Two of these troops formed a squadron, or *epilarchy*; and four squadrons composed a regiment, or *hipparchy*, of 512 men. And the complement of a phalanx was, as we have seen, two of these *hipparchys*, numbering 1024 men and horses, and bearing the proportion of one-sixth of the total infantry of the phalanx.

The grand phalanx was composed of four of these single phalanxes, and may be considered as the command of a general-in-chief.

The double phalanx, composed of two single phalanxes, formed the command of a lieutenant-general;
while the single phalanx may be looked on as the command of a general of division.

It was its compact order which rendered the Macedonian phalanx so formidable in a charge; but such a
body, though well calculated to resist cavalry attack,
would be unsuited to the present day, when its dense
mass would present so favourable a mark to our gunners.

The principal weapon of the phalangite was the pike,
of twenty-four feet in length.   The *sarissa*, as the pike
was called, protruded eighteen feet beyond the man who
presented it, so that one file of the front rank had a
hedge of five bristling spears, besides his own, to protect
him from an enemy.

The formation of the phalanx which was peculiar to
itself, was the *synapism*, in which the soldiers were so
closely jammed together that they could not move, excepting all together in the same direction; the leading
files held their bucklers in front of them, the other
ranks held their bucklers over the heads of those immediately in their front.   By this means the protection
afforded by the bucklers was like that afforded to the
tortoise by its shell, so that it is said a man could run
on the surface of the bucklers as on a roof.   The Romans named one of their military machines " the tortoise," after the *synapism*.

The Greeks practised most of the formations in use
among ourselves, — the line, column, square, echellon;
and they, as well as the Romans, recognised in their
tactics several different orders of battle, which may,

however, all be classed under the head of the *parallel* or the *oblique* order.*

Philip of Macedon commenced, and his son Alexander completed, the organisation of the Macedonian army, on a system not much less elaborate than exists at the present time in the best armies of Europe.

They formed a complete ordnance corps, consisting both of siege and of field artillery.

They established also a transport corps under military officers, furnished with its train of carts, horses, and mules.

It is not to be supposed that the soldiers commanded by Hannibal in the second Punic war were organised precisely in the manner above described. Doubtless the Spaniards and Africans who accompanied him to Italy had been trained to a great extent on that system. But the unwieldy pike had been given up; and after the battle of the Trebbia Hannibal armed his African soldiers in the Roman fashion. The general formation of the phalanx in sixteen ranks, and its various divisions, were still retained; but a greater rapidity of movement was necessarily communicated to it to enable it successfully to oppose the Roman legion.

* For definition of oblique order of battle, see "Theory of War." Maxim 19. p. 151.

See also the chapter on Manœuvres, p. 261. to end of chapter.

INTRODUCTORY CHAPTER.

THE Second Punic war was termed by the historian Livy, the most memorable of all wars that ever were carried on. And there is no exaggeration in the expression, for a parallel to its incidents and achievements, as well as to the great importance of its results, is only to be found in modern history. That great struggle was to determine whether the world was to be ruled by Rome or Carthage.

On this subject the French historian Michelet, in his " Histoire Romaine," has the following passage : —

" It is not without reason that so universal and vivid a remembrance of the Punic wars has dwelt in the memories of men. They formed no mere struggle to determine the lot of two cities or two empires; but it was a strife, on the event of which depended the fate of two races of mankind, whether the dominion of the world should belong to the Indo-Germanic or to the Semitic family of nations. Bear in mind, that the first of these comprises, besides the Indians and the Persians, the Greeks, the Romans, and the Germans. In the other are ranked the Jews and the Arabs, the Phœnicians, and the Carthaginians. On the one side is the genius of heroism, of art, and legislation ; on the other, is the spirit of industry, of commerce, of navigation. The two opposite races have everywhere come into contact, everywhere into hostility. In the primitive history of Persia and Chaldea, the heroes are perpetually engaged in combat with their industrious and perfidious neighbours. The struggle is renewed between the Phœnicians and the Greeks on every coast of the Mediterranean. The Greek supplants the Phœnician in all his factories, all his colonies in the east; soon will the Roman come and do likewise in the west. Alexander did far more against Tyre than Salmanasar or Nebuchodonosor had done. Not content with crushing her, he took care that she never should survive : for he founded Alexandria as her substitute, and changed for ever the track of the commerce of the world. There remained Carthage—the great Carthage and her mighty empire, — mighty in a far different degree than Phœnicia's had been. Rome annihilated it. Then occurred that which has no parallel in history, — an entire civilisation perished at one blow — vanished, like a falling star. The ' Periplus ' of Hanno, a few coins, a score of lines in Plautus, and, lo, all that remains of the Carthaginian world !

"Many generations must needs pass away before the struggle between the two races could be renewed ; and the Arabs, that formidable rear guard of the Semitic world, dashed forth from their deserts. The conflict between the two races then became the conflict of two religions. Fortunate was it that those daring Saracenic cavaliers encountered in the east the impregnable walls of Constantinople, in the west the chivalrous valour of

Charles Martel, and the sword of the Cid.   The crusades
were the natural reprisals for the Arab invasions, and
form the last epoch of that great struggle between the
two principal families of the human race."

In the destruction of Carthage perished almost all the
documents which would have conveyed to posterity a full
idea of the character and institutions of Rome's great
rival.

But we can perceive how inferior Carthage was to
her competitor in military spirit, military resources, and
position; and how far less fitted than Rome she was to
become the founder of a dominion destined to exist for
ages, which should bind together barbarians of every
race and language into an organised empire, and fit
them for becoming, after that empire should be dis-
solved, the free members of the commonwealth of Chris-
tian Europe.

One great source of the inferiority of Carthage was
that she had no native army.   Her citizens were essentially, that which the English have sometimes been
taunted with being—a trading people.

Michelet remarks : " The life of an industrious mer-
chant, of a Carthaginian, was too precious to be risked, as
long as it was possible to substitute advantageously for it
that of a barbarian from Spain or Gaul.   Carthage knew,
and could tell to a drachma, what the life of a man from
each nation came to.   A Greek was worth more than a
Campanian, a Campanian worth more than a Gaul or a
Spaniard.   When once this tariff of blood was correctly
made out, Carthage began a war as a mercantile specu-
lation.   She tried to make conquests in the hope of

getting new mines to work, or to open fresh markets for her exports. In one venture she could afford to spend 50,000 mercenaries, in another rather more. If the returns were good, there was no regret felt for the capital that had been lavished in the investment: more money got more men, and all went on well."

And commenting on this, Professor Creasy, in his most interesting and valuable work on the "Decisive Battles of the World" has the following eloquent passage: —

"Armies composed of mercenaries have, in all ages, been as formidable to their employers as to the enemy against whom they were directed. We know of one occasion (between the first and second Punic wars) when Carthage was brought to the very brink of destruction by a revolt of her foreign troops. Other mutinies of the same kind must from time to time have occurred. Probably one of these was the cause of the comparative weakness of Carthage at the time of the Athenian expedition against Syracuse; so different from the energy with which she attacked Gelon half a century earlier, and Dionysius half a century later. And even when we consider her armies with reference only to their efficiency in warfare, we perceive at once the inferiority of such bands of condottieri, brought together without any common bond of origin, tactics, or cause, to the legions of Rome, which, at the time of the Punic wars, were raised from the very flower of a hardy agricultural population, trained in the strictest discipline, habituated to victory, and animated by the most resolute patriotism. And this shows also the transcendency of the genius of Hannibal, which could form such discordant materials into a compact organised force, and inspire them with the spirit of patient discipline and loyalty to their chief; so that they were true to him in his adverse as well as in his prosperous fortunes, and throughout the chequered series of his campaigns no panic rout ever disgraced a division under his command; no mutiny, or even attempt at mutiny, was ever known in his camp; and, finally, after fifteen years of Italian warfare, his men followed their old leader to Zama, ' with no fear, and little hope;' and there on that disastrous field stood firm around him his old guard, till Scipio's Numidian allies came up on their flank; when at last, surrounded and overpowered, the veteran battalions sealed their devotion to their general with their blood!"

The general appearance of a Carthaginian army has been described by one of the historians of the period as follows:—

"It was an assemblage of the most opposite races of the human species, from the farthest parts of the globe. Hordes of half-naked Gauls were ranged next to companies of white-clothed Iberians, and savage Ligurians next to the far-travelled Nasamones and Lotophagi. Carthaginians and Phœnici-Africans formed the centre; while innumerable troops of Numidian horsemen, taken from all the tribes of the Desert, swarmed about on unsaddled horses, and formed the wings; the van was composed of Balearic slingers; and a line of colossal elephants, with their Ethiopian guides, formed, as it were, a chain of moving fortresses before the whole army."

The Spaniards and Africans were armed with helmets

and shields; and, for offensive weapons, with short cut and thrust swords. But after the battle of Thrasymene Hannibal armed his Spanish and African infantry after the Roman fashion, by means of the arms taken in the battle.

The Gauls carried long javelins, and huge broad swords and targets, similar to those described by Sir Walter Scott as having been the weapons of the Scottish Gael at a more recent period.

In the contest now under consideration, Hannibal's heavy infantry was composed of Spaniards, Africans, and Gauls. His light infantry, of the famous and formidable Balearic slingers and Gaulish irregulars. The only cavalry we read of as having accompanied him into Italy consisted of Numidian irregulars, who were yet very formidable in the field, and the best scouts in the world. But, after his entrance into Italy, Hannibal organised a body of Gaulish heavy cavalry, which did him good service in his subsequent campaigns.

Rome, the iron kingdom of prophecy, was the greatest military power the world has ever seen; conquest was the breath of her nostrils; and her military organisation was the most perfect that has ever existed. The following extract from Gibbon enables us to understand by what means the Roman dominion was extended over the whole of the known world.

" The Roman peasant, or mechanic, imbibed the useful prejudice that he received advancement in being permitted to enter the more dignified profession of arms, in which his rank and reputation would depend on his own valour; and that, although the prowess of a private soldier must often escape the notice of fame, his own behaviour might sometimes confer glory or disgrace on the company, the legion, or even the army, to whose honours he was associated. On his first entrance into the service, an oath was administered to him with every circumstance of solemnity. He promised never to desert his standard, to submit his own will to the commands of his leaders, and to sacrifice his life for the safety of the emperor and the empire. The attachment of the Roman troops to their standards was inspired by the united influence of religion and of honour. The golden eagle, which glittered in the front of the legion, was the object of their fondest devotion; nor was it esteemed less impious than it was ignominious to abandon that sacred ensign in the hour of danger. These motives, which derived their strength from the imagination, were enforced by fears and hopes of a more substantial kind. Regular pay, occasional donatives, and a stated recompense after the appointed time of service, alleviated the hardships of the military life, whilst, on the other hand, it was impossible for cowardice or disobedience to escape the severest punishment. The centurions were authorised to chastise with blows, the generals had a right to punish with death; and it was an inflexible maxim of Roman discipline that a good soldier should dread his officers far more than the enemy. From such laudable arts did the valour of the imperial troops receive a degree of firmness and docility, unattainable by the impetuous and irregular passions of barbarians.

"And yet so sensible were the Romans of the imperfection of valour without skill and practice, that, in their language, the name of an army was borrowed from the word which signified exercise. Military exercises were the important and unremitted object of their discipline. The recruits and young soldiers were constantly trained, both in the morning and in the evening; nor was age or knowledge allowed to excuse the veterans from the daily repetition of what they had completely learnt. Large sheds were erected in the winter-quarters of the troops, that their useful labours might not receive any interruption from the most tempestuous weather; and it was carefully observed that the arms destined to this imitation of war should be of double the weight which was required in real action. It is not the purpose of this work to enter into any minute description of the Roman exercises. We shall only remark that they comprehend whatever could add strength to the body, activity to the limbs, or grace to the motions. The soldiers were diligently instructed to march, to run, to leap, to swim, to carry heavy burdens, to handle every species of arms that was used either for offence or for defence, either in distant engagement or in a closer onset; to form a variety of evolutions; and to move to the sound of flutes in the Pyrrhic or martial dance. In the midst of peace, the Roman troops familiarised themselves with the practice of war; and it is prettily remarked by an ancient historian, who had fought against them, that the effusion of blood was the only circumstance which distinguished a field of battle from a field of exercise. It was the policy of the ablest generals, and even of the emperors themselves, to encourage these military studies by their presence and example; and we are informed that Hadrian as well as Trajan, frequently condescended to instruct the inexperienced soldiers, to reward the diligent, and sometimes to dispute with them the prize of superior strength or dexterity."

In our own day, and in our own country, we may congratulate ourselves in having at the head of the army a royal prince, who has given the strongest evidence of his disposition to encourage, and even to enforce, all necessary military studies and exercises; and as the British soldier is in nowise inferior to the Roman legionary in strength, courage, or devotion, there is little doubt that, although we are not a military people, if the earnestness and energy of the commander-in-chief be only emulated by his officers, the English army will have no reason to dread a comparison with any force either of ancient or modern days.

CHAPTER I.

MARCH INTO ITALY AND FIRST CAMPAIGN.

HANNIBAL, the son of Hamilcar, surnamed Barca, or the thunderbolt, was with his father in Spain during the interval which elapsed between the first and second Punic wars; and he was only nine years old at the time when he took that famous oath of enmity against Rome, which he so religiously kept in after life.

Hannibal commanded the Carthaginian armies in Spain with uninterrupted success for nine years. The expedition to that country was originally undertaken at his instance, because he foresaw that no long time could elapse before Rome and Carthage would again be enemies.

He was sensible that Carthage was weak, in consequence of her having no native army; and he designed not only to train his existing army in a constant warfare against the bravest of barbarians, but to effect permanent conquests in Spain. It was his policy to attach the new subjects to the mother city by kind treatment, at the same time that he conciliated the native independent Princes; and he hoped thus not only to ensure a constant supply of good soldiers to recruit his armies, but, by gaining possession of the productive gold and silver mines of the south of the Peninsula, to obtain the means of paying them.

Hamilcar was slain in battle in the year B.C. 229, it is supposed in the country between the Tagus and Douro rivers, to which he had pushed his conquests. Hasdrubal, his son-in-law, appears to have inherited not only his command, but also his spirit and genius. He consolidated the conquests of Hamilcar, no less by his policy than by the engaging influence of his personal manners and character; and he accommodated himself so successfully to the feelings and habits of the Spaniards, which he had carefully studied with that view, that the native chiefs, far and near, vied with each other in their eagerness to become the allies of Carthage.

Rome watched the progress of Hasdrubal with uneasiness; and as the threatening of a Gaulic invasion at that time rendered it inexpedient to have recourse to arms, she endeavoured to secure herself by a treaty, the provisions of which bound Hasdrubal not to push his conquests beyond the Iberus, and obliged each of the contracting parties to abstain from molesting the allies of the other. The city of Saguntum had lately placed itself under the protection of Rome, and was therefore, by the terms of the treaty, secure from attack, although situated so far south of the Iberus. The Romans hoped doubtless by its means, to obtain a more forward footing in Spain, from which, when the Gaulic war should be terminated, they might sap the newly formed dominion of Carthage in that country.

Hasdrubal was assassinated in the year 221 B.C., after a successful administration of the affairs of Spain during eight years; and now Hannibal, at the early age of twenty-four, by the unanimous voice of the soldiers, was called to the chief command of the Carthaginian forces in Spain; and the Senate of Carthage ratified the choice of the army. Two years were occupied with expeditions against the native tribes of the interior; but in the third year Hannibal, having matured his plans, resolved to provoke a war with Rome by besieging Saguntum.* He accordingly laid siege to that city, and although left entirely to its own resources by its covenanted protectors, it was no sooner taken, after a heroic defence of eight months, than the Romans sent ambassadors to Carthage to demand that Hannibal and his principal officers should be delivered up to them for their infraction of the treaty.

In default of compliance with that demand the second Punic war was declared B.C. 218.

This short introduction has been necessary in order to convey a clear understanding of the progress of that great struggle; for it will be seen that the event was materially influenced by the operations in Spain at different periods of the contest.

Long before the declaration of war, Hannibal had been maturing in his own mind his great project of the invasion of Italy; and had neglected no measure which could conduce to its success. He had sent emissaries through Gaul and across the Alps into Cisalpine Gaul, in order to sound the disposition of the inhabitants

* See Observation 1.

along the route he proposed to follow, and to secure for his army a friendly reception from the Cisalpine Gauls on its descent from the Alps. He well knew the character of that lively and fickle people and their hatred of the Romans; and he trusted to his own genius, to convert their country into a secure base of operations, and themselves into active and faithful allies.

It was late in the month of May, B.C. 218, that Hannibal set out from New Carthage on his great undertaking; and "thus," in the beautiful language of Arnold, "with no divided heart and with an entire resignation of all personal and domestic enjoyments for ever, Hannibal went forth, at the age of twenty-seven, to do the work of his country's gods, and to redeem his early vow."

The force with which he quitted New Carthage amounted to 90,000 foot and 12,000 horse. He crossed the Iberus and might have advanced without loss of time to the Pyrenees; but the country between the Iberus and those mountains was friendly to the Romans, some of its towns held Roman garrisons, it therefore became necessary to subdue this district entirely, and thereby to deprive the Romans of a convenient base of operations from which they might otherwise attack the Carthaginian conquests in Spain.

Hannibal effected this object speedily, though with great loss of life; and having left Hanno with 11,000 men to guard his new conquest, and sent an equal number of his Spanish soldiers back to their homes*, he crossed the Pyrenees and entered Gaul with an

* See Observation 2.

army which was now reduced by these detachments and the losses it had sustained in the field, to 50,000 foot and 9000 horse.

From the Pyrenees to the Rhone his progress was easy, an unmolested passage through their territories being purchased by presents to the native chiefs. But the passage of the Rhone was not to be effected without opposition, for the city of Massilia (the modern Marseilles) was a fast ally of Rome, and its influence had been successfully exerted with the neighbouring tribes of the eastern bank to induce them to oppose the progress of the invader. Besides this, P. Scipio, one of the Roman consuls for the year, had lately arrived off the mouth of the Rhone with a fleet and army on his way to Spain; and learning there that Hannibal had actually passed the Pyrenees, he disembarked his force, with the intention of opposing him on the Rhone, and in the hope of preventing his advance beyond that river.

Hannibal in his march through Gaul kept his army as far as possible away from the sea-coast, in order to conceal his movements from the Romans; and Scipio, hearing nothing of him, and believing that his progress must necessarily be slow, lingered at the mouth of the Rhone at the very time when the friendly tribes of the eastern bank were vainly endeavouring to prevent Hannibal's passage of the river. Scipio contented himself with sending forth 300 light cavalry to ascend the left bank and to endeavour to gain some information of the movements of the invading army.*

Hannibal is supposed to have struck the Rhone at a

* See Observation 3.

point about half way between its mouth and its confluence with the Isara (the modern Isère). He immediately purchased all their boats and vessels of every
kind from the inhabitants of the western shore, and
having constructed others of the timber which abounded
on the spot, he in two days possessed sufficient transport to ferry his whole army across the river. But he
found the Gauls of the opposite shore assembled to
oppose his passage, and his dispositions to effect it are
well worthy of attention.

He sent off a strong detachment by night, with native
guides, to ascend the river for about twenty miles, and
then to cross as best they could, where there would be
no enemy to oppose them. This detachment selected a
part of the river where its course was divided into two
narrow channels by an island, and there effected the
passage without difficulty by means of rafts constructed
of the timber which was found on the spot.

Hannibal, by previous concert, waited forty-eight
hours from the time when the detachment left him,
and then on the third morning from that time made all
his preparations for the passage of his main body. The
first division was assembled in the boats and only
awaited the signal agreed upon to push off. That signal was the smoke of a great fire kindled by the detachment which had crossed the river, and which had now
marched down to within a short distance of the barbarians on the opposite bank, whose whole attention
was engrossed by the sight of Hannibal's preparations,
and who crowded down to all the accessible parts of the
river shore to oppose his landing. The first division

now pushed off. The Rhone was full and rapid. The largest and heaviest vessels were placed highest up stream to serve as a breakwater to the others. The men pulled vigorously against the current, and as the flotilla approached the opposite bank the attention of the Gauls was directed to a mass of fire which appeared in their rear, and now the detachments which had kindled it charged upon their right flank and rear, at the same time that the flotilla stranded; and the soldiers, at whose head was Hannibal, leaping ashore, attacked the bewildered barbarians in front. These made a feeble resistance, and fled in confusion. The boats were instantly sent back for the second division, and before nightfall Hannibal's whole army, with the exception of the elephants, was encamped on the eastern bank of the Rhone.

Early next morning Hannibal sent out some Numidians to ascertain the position of Scipio's army. Not many hours elapsed before these horsemen were seen returning to the camp, as if riding for their lives from a pursuing enemy. They had indeed fallen in with the light cavalry sent out by Scipio, who had attacked and driven in the Numidians, and who now, as soon as they came in sight of the Carthaginian camp, wheeled about to carry back tidings to their general.

Scipio now no longer delayed to put his army in motion to oppose Hannibal, but he was already too late, for when he reached the place which had been the site of the Carthaginian camp, he learnt that Hannibal had quitted it three days before and had marched northwards up the Rhone. To have followed him through an unknown country, whose inhabitants, as Gauls, probably hated the Roman name, would have been madness; for it must be remembered that the tribes which opposed him on the Rhone were in the neighbourhood and under the influence of Massilia.

Scipio, therefore, perceiving it was no longer possible to prevent Hannibal from reaching the Alps, resolved to meet him in Italy on his descent from those mountains, when he hoped that the Carthaginian army, exhausted by the fatigues and privations inseparable from such a march, and diminished in numbers, would be easily vanquished by the Roman forces which were already assembled in Cisalpine Gaul.*

Scipio accordingly again descended the Rhone, and having despatched his army to Spain under the command of his brother, Cnæus Scipio, as his lieutenant, sailed himself to Pisa, whence he proceeded across the Apennines to take command of the Roman legions which were stationed on the Po under the Prætors Manlius and Atilius, whose force amounted to about 25,000 men.

Meanwhile, on the day after the sudden apparition of the Roman cavalry, Hannibal, having with some difficulty effected the passage of the elephants, broke up his camp and marched northwards, covering the rear of his line of march with his cavalry and elephants; for he believed Scipio to be in his immediate neighbourhood, and expected to be pursued.

The precise direction of his march is uncertain, but it appears probable that after having espoused the cause of one of two brothers near Valance who contended for

* See Observation 4.

the chieftainship of their tribe, and having received from the successful competitor in return important succours, in the shape of provisions, arms, clothing, and above all of shoes,—the Carthaginian army crossed the Isère, and still proceeding for some distance up the left bank of the Rhone, at length struck off to the right across the plains of Dauphiné and reached the first ascent of the Alps.

This was near the northern extremity of that ridge of limestone mountains which, rising suddenly out of the plains to a height of 5000 feet, fills up the space between the Rhone at Belley and the Isère below Grenoble, and separates the plains of Dauphiné from the rich and wide valley extending from the Lake of Bourget to the Isère at Montmeillan. At the place where Hannibal crossed this ridge, it is of no great width. His progress was opposed by the natives, who guarded the defiles through which he must pass; but, learning that these only guarded them during the day, and at night withdrew to their homes in the valley beyond, he seized the defiles after nightfall, and on the next day effected the passage of his army, not without being attacked, however, and penetrated into the valley of Montmeillan. This town he took by storm. It was the principal stronghold of the barbarians, and in it he found large supplies of provisions and cattle.

Halting there for one day to rest his men, he then proceeded for three days up the right bank of the Isère. He was now met by a deputation of the natives who professed to be friendly, and having received from them supplies and hostages for their good behaviour, he was induced, by their plausible conduct, to accept of their guidance through a difficult part of the mountains to which he was approaching.   Here he narrowly escaped destruction from an attack made upon him by his treacherous friends at the most difficult part of the way; but at length all obstacles were surmounted, and on the ninth day after quitting the plains of Dauphiné, Hannibal and his army stood on the summit of the central ridge of the Alps, supposed to be the summit of the little St. Bernard Pass.

The period of the year was about the end of October; the first winter snows had already fallen; and the climate of the country being far more severe than at present, owing to the dense forests which at that time covered the face of Germany, Hannibal's southern soldiers must have been in dreary quarters. It is probable that great numbers perished from cold, and certain that all must have been much worn and disheartened; for many mountain peaks still rose between them and Italy, through which their descent was likely to be both perilous and painful.   But Hannibal's ascendancy over his men was complete ; and, after a rest of two days, he resumed his march.

No more open hostility was manifested by the natives, but the natural difficulties of the route were greater than ever. The snow concealed the track, so that many losing it, fell over frightful precipices.   At last the army came to a place where the track had been carried away by an avalanche for a distance of 300 yards.   It was impossible to turn this obstacle by scaling the heights above, on account of the great depth of snow; and nothing remained but to reconstruct the road.

A summit of some extent was found and cleared of snow, on which the army encamped, and all, working for their lives, succeeded in completing in one day a practicable road for the cavalry and baggage animals, which were immediately sent on to encamp in a valley beyond; but for the passage of the elephants a wider and more solid way was required, and its construction occupied two days more, during which both men and elephants suffered terribly from cold and want.

At length all passed safely, and after a further toilsome march of three days, the army cleared the mountains and entered the territory of the Insubrian Gauls, messengers from whom had previously met Hannibal on the Rhone, to assure him of a friendly reception in their country.

The valley by which Hannibal is supposed to have descended into Italy, is the Dorea Baltea, the same by which Napoleon penetrated with his famous army of reserve in the Marengo campaign.

The principal difficulties of this march arose from the lateness of the season. Had the summit of the little St. Bernard been reached a month earlier, no fresh snow would have fallen, and fodder might have been procured for the cattle without difficulty. The commissariat labours must have been very great, as provisions had to be carried for about 30,000 men and 8000 cavalry horses, besides what was required for the baggage and pack animals, which could not have numbered less than 5000 or 6000.

Hannibal carried with him out of the mountains only 12,000 African and 8000 Spanish infantry, the remnant of 50,000 with which he quitted Spain. His cavalry, too, had dwindled from 9000 to 6000 horses.

He gave his army the rest its exhausted condition required, and having recruited its strength, his first expedition was undertaken against the Taurinians of Liguria who were hostile to the Insubrians, and would not on that account listen to the proposals of Hannibal to join him against the Romans. He took and sacked their chief city, Augusta (the same as modern Turin), and struck such terror into the neighbouring tribes that they submitted and became his allies.

It is now time to turn our attention to the preparations the Romans had been making in the interval between Hannibal's departure from Spain and his arrival in Italy, and to the forces they had assembled to oppose their great enemy.

The two consuls of the year were, P. Scipio and Ti. Sempronius. Scipio's province was Spain, and it has been already related how, after his unsuccessful endeavour to stop Hannibal on the Rhone, he despatched his army to that province, while he himself went to command on the Po.

Sempronius, with another consular army, was destined to cross over into Sicily, and thence, if circumstances were favourable, to make a descent on Africa, in the hope by threatening Carthage to recall Hannibal to its defence. But Hannibal had not neglected among his other preparations to provide against such a contingency. Before he quitted Spain, fresh troops were, at his suggestion, sent to that country from Africa, to be commanded during his absence by his brother Hasdrubal, while he sent Spanish troops to defend the territory of Carthage, in order that the soldiers of each nation, being quartered among foreigners, should be deprived of the temptation, or the opportunity to revolt.

He was also, in all probability, actuated by the consideration that his bitterest enemies were to be found in that faction of his fellow citizens which was headed by Hanno. And he was, therefore, not sorry to hold that faction in check by the presence of a force which, on account of its personal attachment to himself, owed an allegiance to Hannibal rather than to Carthage.

A third army, consisting, like the two first, of two Roman legions and the usual proportion of allies, and amounting to about 20,000 men, was sent to Cisalpine Gaul under the Prætor L. Manlius; and in order further to restrain the disaffected Gauls, the military colonists of two Roman colonies to the number of 12,000 men, were despatched to occupy the important posts of Placentia and Cremona, on opposite sides of the Po. Thus the Roman force which was actually assembled in Cisalpine Gaul so early as the end of May of the year 218, amounted to 32,000 men and was considered amply sufficient to preserve tranquillity. But before Scipio had set out from Rome to assume his consular command, news arrived that the Boian and Insubrian Gauls had risen, that they had defeated Manlius and blockaded him in one of his towns, and that they had moreover dispersed the colonists of Placentia and Cremona, and driven them to take refuge in Mutina, another Roman colony on the road between Placentia and Ariminum.

One of Scipio's legions was immediately sent off under another prætor, Caius Atilius, to relieve and reinforce Manlius, while Scipio's army was raised to its original strength by new levies.

Thus when Scipio arrived in Cisalpine Gaul, towards the end of the year, he found the army of the prætors in the field amounting to about 25,000 men, and the military colonists re-established in Placentia and Cremona; and it was of this aggregate force that he took the command.

It was now the middle of December, and unusually late for military operations, but Scipio being anxious by a rapid advance to prevent a general rising of the Gauls in favour of Hannibal, crossed the Po at Placentia, and marched up its northern bank; while Hannibal on the other hand knowing well that the Gauls were prevented from joining him by fear alone, and certain that his first success against the Roman arms would draw multitudes to his standard, descended the northern bank to meet Scipio, who, having crossed the Ticinus by a bridge he had constructed, continued to advance westward with the river on his left.

Thus was brought on accidentally a cavalry action, which has been magnified by the name of the battle of the Ticinus, in which the Numidians, supported by the Gaulish heavy cavalry, completely defeated the Roman horse, and in which Scipio himself was dangerously wounded. Here was first established the superiority of the cavalry of Hannibal over that of the Romans, to which he owed much of his subsequent success; and the country being level and open, and peculiarly favourable to the action of that arm in which they were so evidently inferior, the Romans retired behind the Ticinus, over the bridge which they had made, and which they now broke down behind them; but this operation was attended with so much confusion that 600 men were left on the wrong side of the river, and fell into the hands of the enemy.

Hannibal, not judging it prudent to attempt the passage of such a river as the Ticinus in the face of the Romans, retraced his steps up the northern bank of the Po until he found a convenient place, where he trans-ported his army to the southern bank by means of the river boats. The Romans now fearing to be turned, and lest Hannibal should reach Placentia before them, retreated in all haste on that city and encamped under its walls.

Hannibal marching down the Po came in sight of the Roman camp two days after crossing the river, and after vainly endeavouring to provoke the enemy to an engagement, he placed his army about five miles to the south-east of Placentia, cutting off Scipio's communica-tion with Ariminum and Rome.* Hannibal was here in a friendly country, for, as he expected would be the case, he was received with open arms by the natives on the south of the Po, and indeed the Romans had no hold on the territory of Cisalpine Gaul but by their garrisons or colonies.

Hannibal's appearance in Italy took the Roman senate by surprise. They judged that the difficulties

* See Observation 5.

of the march must delay his arrival until the following spring. But they no sooner received intelligence that he was actually in Cisalpine Gaul than they sent for Sempronius and his army from Sicily, and despatched them to reinforce Scipio on the Po.

Sempronius was with his army at Lilybæum, the furthest point of Sicily, when he received his orders; and it may give a small idea of the immensely increased facilities which science has imparted to military operations, that rather than encounter the dangers of a winter navigation — instead of embarking at Lilybæum and sailing to Ariminum, the troops marched through Sicily to Messana, there crossed the straits, and proceeded through the whole length of Italy by Ariminum to the scene of conflict on the Po, which they reached in about forty days. In our time the operation would probably be effected in four.

Sempronius effected his junction with Scipio unimpeded by Hannibal, and the army of the consuls then moving westward crossed to the left bank of the Trebbia, where it encamped. This movement was probably made by the Romans in order to draw near the magazines, of which they possessed several south of the Po, and on which they depended for their subsistence; for, as it has been already remarked, they had no hold on the country excepting by their garrisons, and without these the Roman army might have starved while Hannibal had all his wants amply supplied by the goodwill of the inhabitants.

The army of the consuls amounted to about 40,000 men; and that of Hannibal had been so reinforced by the accession of the Gauls since its descent from the Alps, that it was little, if at all, inferior in numbers. It was Hannibal's policy to bring on a decisive battle as soon as possible. It is true the Gauls were friendly and furnished all his wants; but they were proverbially fickle, they were impatient to share in the plunder of Roman territory, and they would naturally chafe at a delay, the effect of which was to throw the burden of supporting the Carthaginian army exclusively upon them.

To force the Romans to a battle Hannibal attacked their magazines. One of the principal of these, Clastidium, was betrayed into his hands by the treachery of its governor; and in it he found large supplies of corn. After this, the Carthaginian army encamped on the right bank of the Trebbia, opposite to and within sight of the Roman camp. As Scipio was still disabled by his wound received at the Ticinus, the sole command of the Roman army devolved on Sempronius, who was no less eager to fight than Hannibal; and he is not to be censured for rashness in desiring to bring on an engagement,— for the hostile armies were equal in strength, and Hannibal's transcendent genius was as yet unproved,— but for the entire disregard of all military rules he evinced in conducting the operation.

Early in the morning, Hannibal sent his Numidians across the river to skirmish with the Roman horse, and, if possible, to entice the Romans by retreating to cross the river in pursuit. He had previously posted his brother Mago with 2000 picked men in an ambush, in the overgrown bed of a watercourse, in such a position that, when passed by the Romans in their advance after crossing the river, Mago might burst out upon their flank and rear, while Hannibal engaged them in front.

Sempronius fell into the snare; he ordered first his cavalry and then his whole army to follow the flying Numidians across the river.   It was mid-winter, bitterly cold, and the stream ran breast high.   It is said the Romans had not broken their fast, and thus wet, exhausted, and half-frozen, Sempronius after crossing formed his troops in order of battle with the river in their rear.*

Meanwhile Hannibal's men had breakfasted and formed leisurely to meet the enemy's attack.

The Romans as was their custom were formed in three lines, with the cavalry, only 4000 strong, on the flanks, in the order which has been described in the introductory remarks.

Hannibal drew up his army in two lines.   In the first were his light troops and Balearic slingers.   The second line was composed of his heavy-armed African, Spanish, and Gaulish infantry, amounting to about 20,000 men.

The elephants and the cavalry, 10,000 strong, were divided between the wings.

The battle was opened as usual by the light troops; and the Roman Velites, already exhausted with their morning work, were soon driven through the intervals of the maniples to the rear.   The Roman cavalry too, charged by the elephants and by the greatly superior

* See Observation 6.

hostile cavalry, was broken immediately and driven off the field. But when the Roman infantry came to close, their courage and discipline seemed capable of restoring the balance; but at this critical moment Mago's ambush burst on their rear, while the victorious Carthaginian cavalry, which had returned from the pursuit of the Roman horse, charged both their flanks, and Hannibal pressed them in front. No troops could withstand such an onset. The centre legions indeed, commanded by Sempronius, overbearing all opposition, burst through their opponents and marched clear off the field to Placentia *; but the remainder were driven back into the Trebbia with tremendous slaughter.

Only a small remnant reached the opposite bank, and Scipio, after nightfall, leading this remnant once more across the river, passed the enemy in the dark, and joined his colleague within the walls of Placentia.

Thus ended Hannibal's first campaign in Italy.

See Observations 7 and 8.

OBSERVATIONS ON THE FOREGOING CHAPTER.

1. Hannibal's sagacity is evidenced by his resolution to provoke a war with Rome. He was well aware of the moral force which attaches generally to the initiative in war; and he perceived also that the relative circumstances of the two powers lent a particular value to the initiative in the present instance. In the first Punic war all the success had been on the side of the Romans and the tide of fortune had set in too strongly in their favour to admit of its being turned by the genius of Hamilcar, who was advanced to the command of the Carthaginian armies too late for that purpose. In consequence of their successes in that war, Hannibal calculated that the Romans, reposing in a haughty security, would be very slow to believe that their despised enemies would willingly engage with them in a second struggle. Hence the Roman apathy in permitting Saguntum to fall, without any more active attempt at its relief than the remonstrance of an envoy. Hence also the time that was lost to Rome, and gained by Hannibal for his preparations, in sending ambassadors to Carthage to demand an explanation after the fall of Saguntum, in place of immediately declaring war and accompanying that declaration with an invasion of Africa, for which purpose Sicily would have served as a convenient stepping-stone and base of operations.

Such an energetic proceeding on the part of Rome would have occasioned the recall of all the Carthaginian forces from Spain, and the consequent loss of all the fruits of the Carthaginian conquests in that country; and Carthage would have commenced the war much in the same relative position as that which she occupied at the beginning of the first Punic war.

On the other hand, if the Carthaginians took the initiative, all the advantages would be for them. Hannibal calculated that if he could once cross the Alps with an army, he could so work upon the hatred to Rome which was the universal feeling among the Cisalpine Gauls, as to convert that fickle people into zealous allies, and their territory into a base for his subsequent operations; he hoped also to derive advantage from the constitution of the different states of Italy which were in alliance with and dependent on the Roman Republic. Though called by the name of allies, they were in reality subjects, and although the existing generation in those states had grown up in peace with the Romans, their constrained alliance had not quite extinguished the old feelings of hatred and rivalry.

Hannibal counted on the influence of those feelings, combined with the prestige of the victories he hoped to gain, to aid in detaching the allies from their fidelity, and to isolate the Roman republic proper in the midst of a surrounding hostile population. He saw that all depended on the initiative, and that, if he could once gain a footing in Italy, as it were by surprise, he might afford to disregard any diversion his enemies might attempt to make by threatening Carthage.

2. It has been related that immediately before he crossed the Pyrenees, Hannibal sent about 11,000 of his Spanish soldiers back to their homes. This measure is an instance of that great knowledge of human nature, which alone could have enabled him for so many years to rule an army composed of such discordant materials, so that, " throughout the chequered series of his campaigns, no mutiny or even attempt at mutiny was ever known in his camp." The explanation is as follows : — in the march to the Pyrenees, about 3000 Spaniards, frightened by the perils of the enterprise, deserted. Hannibal, sensible of the impolicy of attempting to prevent further desertion by severe measures which would indicate distrust, and feeling that unwilling troops weaken rather than strengthen an army, gave out that he had himself sent the deserters to their homes as a reward for faithful service ; and gave leave to 8000 more on whom he could least depend, to follow their comrades.

He thus took away the great inducement to depart, at the same time that he rid himself of doubtful followers, whose bad spirit might have inoculated the remainder. This proceeding is one instance of the great value set upon moral agents in war, not only by Hannibal, but by every one who has the least pretension to be called a great general.

3. Scipio's apathy in remaining quietly at the mouth of the Rhone, after he had ascertained that Hannibal

had actually entered Gaul, is not to be excused. No pains should have been spared by him to discover the position of the enemy, and the probable line of his advance. He should have sent out his light cavalry to scour the country on the western bank of the Rhone, to bring him intelligence of the approach of Hannibal in sufficient time to enable him to co-operate with the friendly tribes of the eastern bank, in defending the passage of the river. To facilitate this object it was necessary to occupy as central a position as possible. Probably one about midway between the sea and the Isara would have been best chosen.

When it is required to defend a long line, suppose the line of a river, and the point at which an enemy may approach it is uncertain, the general of the defensive force should not attempt to guard every practicable point of passage, for that would be impossible; and, even though it were possible, such a proceeding would too much disseminate his force, and would expose the separated fractions to be beaten in detail, supposing the enemy to succeed, as it is most probable he would do, in effecting his passage somewhere. In such a case the general of the defensive force should keep his troops well in hand in some central position, lining the banks with his light troops to observe the approach and the intentions of the enemy. It should then be his aim to come down suddenly on the enemy while in the act of forming his bridge, or, better still, after a part only of his force should have crossed.

Failing in this, he should previously have named some convenient point of concentration in rear of his general line, commanding the line by which the enemy must advance, where the defensive army, in a strong position, might successfully dispute the further advance of the enemy, and defeat him with the river in his rear.

Had Scipio occupied such a central position as has been supposed in the first instance, and failing thereby to prevent the Carthaginian army from crossing the Rhone, had he concentrated his force in a strong position in the rear, Hannibal could not have reached the Alps without fighting a battle. It was the Roman game to oblige Hannibal to fight as often as possible at a distance from Italy, and thereby to cripple him before he could reach the theatre of his intended operations.

The passage of a great river in presence of an enemy is a great military operation. It may be effected either by main force, or by stratagem in deceiving the enemy as to the intended point of passage; or, as Hannibal here exemplified, by a combination of both.

In general, the passage of a great river which is defended by an enemy, is effected either by stratagem, or by force and stratagem combined.

In such a case, having divided the enemy's attention by demonstrations made by your light troops at various points along the river front, and having attracted his particular notice to some false point by manœuvres calculated to that end, you should then direct your columns as rapidly as possible on the real point previously selected, and throw your bridge across.

Alexander's passage of the Hydaspes is a striking illustration of these remarks; and there is a resemblance between that operation and Hannibal's passage of the Rhone, inasmuch as, in both cases, the first passage was won by troops detached to a distance from the main body, which afterwards moved down on the flank of the defensive force.

4. The resolution which Scipio took to send his army to Spain, its original destination, instead of carrying it back with him to Italy, shows that he was possessed of some of the qualities which go to make up a great general; particularly of that enlarged general view without which a man may be an excellent tactician, but can never become a great commander. It is probably one of the rarest qualities of a general, the power of classifying in his own mind the various events and circumstances which may influence the fate of a campaign, and giving to each no more than its due weight. It is to this faculty the great Napoleon alludes, when he says : " The first quality of a general-in-chief is to have a cool head which receives only a just impression of objects; he should not allow himself to be dazzled either by good or bad news. The sensations which he receives successively or simultaneously in the course of a day, should be classed in his memory so as only to occupy the just place due to each ; for reason and judgment are the resultant of the correct comparison of many sensations. There are some men who, on account of their physical and moral condition, make a single picture to themselves of every event ; whatever knowledge, wit, courage, and other qualities they may possess, nature has not called them to the command of armies and the direction of great military operations."

Scipio foresaw that if the Carthaginians were unopposed in Spain and had leisure to consolidate and to organise their conquests there, the safety of Rome would always be threatened, notwithstanding that Hannibal's army might be expelled from Italy; for the productive gold and silver mines of the Peninsula would constantly replenish the Carthaginian treasury; while the inhabitants, the best and bravest of barbarians, who were capable of becoming under the training of Hannibal and his brother equal to the best soldiers in the world, would afford a constant supply of recruits to the Carthaginian armies.

Arnold says, " Had Publius Scipio, at this critical juncture, not sent his army to Spain instead of carrying it back with him to Italy, his son would in all probability never have won the battle of Zama."

And indeed the progress of this narrative will demonstrate it to be more than probable that if the Carthaginian forces, which were occupied in withstanding the Roman legions in Spain, had been at liberty to reinforce Hannibal in Italy, Rome could not have maintained the contest.

5. The position which Hannibal took up to the southeast of Placentia, between the Roman army and Ariminum, would have been in violation of the rules of war, if Hannibal had not been in a friendly country, and therefore able to march and encamp in any direction, secure of obtaining supplies from the country people. The violation of military rules would have consisted in this, that, although Hannibal had placed himself on the enemy's communications with Rome, the Roman army

was based on Placentia, and had moreover several magazines in the neighbourhood from which it could draw its subsistence, while its position intercepted Hannibal's communications with the country of the Insubrian Gauls, to which he must have looked as his base if the country south of the Po had not been also friendly.

But under the circumstances it was a masterly manœuvre, for Hannibal thereby placed himself between Scipio and the advancing army of Sempronius; and he doubtless did so with the intention of intercepting the latter and of destroying him before he could unite with Scipio. Why he did not execute that intention it is impossible to explain. We learn that Sempronius marched from Ariminum and effected his junction with Scipio near Placentia. We know that Hannibal could not have been restrained by the weakness of his force, because he shortly after engaged the two consuls united; and he ought not to have failed from ignorance of the march of Sempronius, for he possessed a numerous and excellent light cavalry in the Numidians, who were the best scouts in the world. Whatever the explanation may be of his permitting Sempronius to pass him and to join Scipio, if it proceeded from any fault of his, which is very improbable, he speedily redeemed it.

6. The conduct of Sempronius at the battle of the Trebbia is a remarkable instance of military incapacity. In war it is an axiom that every possible chance should be enlisted on your side. But the generalship of Sempronius arrayed every chance against him. Instead of leading into action men fresh and vigorous, his soldiers

fatigued with struggling through the deep cold water, fasting and nearly frozen, were launched against Hannibal's troops in the full vigour of their strength. This was "taking the bull by the horns" with a vengeance; and the river, which the Romans crossed to engage the enemy, added immensely to their losses when they recrossed it to escape from him. It is a maxim that you should never fight with a river or defile in your rear, because, although you may be victorious, in such a position defeat would be ruin; and it is conceivable that even your chances of success would be diminished thereby, as men are not likely to fight so freely when they know their retreat is not secure.

7. The bravery and discipline of the Roman infantry, which broke through the enemy and marched clear off the field to Placentia, were admirable. With Hannibal's numerous cavalry it is difficult to understand how he allowed this body to reach Placentia—it certainly seems that he should have prevented its doing so. A parallel to this march is to be found in the magnificent retreat of the three regiments of the light division under Crawford, across the plain of Fuentes Onoro, in the face of an overwhelming French force of 5000 cavalry, 15 guns, and a large body of infantry in support.

8. The confidence Hannibal felt in the superiority of his own genius, is manifested by his plan for fighting at the Trebbia.

In judging of ordinary men we should be inclined to censure the inactivity which permitted the Roman army to cross the river and to form leisurely on the bank, without taking advantage of the confusion necessarily occasioned by such an operation, to attack and defeat it when landing before it could recover from that confusion. A general less self-confident than Hannibal, when about to engage his troops against an untried enemy, would have availed himself of the above most obvious and certain method of inflicting defeat. But Hannibal's policy was not only to defeat but to destroy, and by the moral effect of the annihilation of his foe to intimidate the Romans, at the same time that he thereby confirmed his new found allies in the belief that they would consult their best interests by remaining faithful to him. Had Hannibal attacked the Romans during their passage of the river their defeat would not have been less certain, but it would have been less decisive both in fact and in its moral effect. A much smaller number of Romans would have fallen; and both they and Hannibal's allies might have entertained, the one the boast, the other the reflection, that had the terrible Roman legions been arrayed against Hannibal on a fair field the result might have been very different.

CHAP. II.

SECOND CAMPAIGN.

AFTER the defeat of the Trebbia the remnant of the Roman army shut itself up in Placentia, and left the open country to Hannibal, who cut off all communication with Etruria and Ariminum. The Romans could only obtain supplies by the Po, east of Placentia, the navigation of which was secured to them by the small town of Emparium, well fortified and strongly garrisoned. This place Hannibal endeavoured to take by a night surprise, but the defenders were on the alert, and having warned the garrison of Placentia by signals previously agreed upon, Scipio marched out of that town at the head of his cavalry followed as closely as possible by his infantry, and attacked the Carthaginians, who, discouraged by a slight wound received by Hannibal, retreated.

To remove the unfavourable moral effect of this failure Hannibal now undertook an expedition against Vicumviæ, a town on the frontiers of Liguria, which the Romans had fortified during the Gaulish war, both for the purposes of a depôt and to act as a check upon the Ligurians. Although he was in possession of Clastidium which served him as a *place d'armes*, Vicumviæ impeded his communications with Liguria, and he therefore took that place by assault.

The consuls despairing of maintaining themselves on the Po, where they were isolated in the midst of a hostile population, took advantage of Hannibal's absence to withdraw from Placentia; and, having separated their forces, Scipio retired to Ariminum, Sempronius across the Apennines into Etruria, where he established his winter-quarters in the neighbourhood of Lucca.* By this measure they hoped to cover both the roads which led from Cisalpine Gaul into the heart of Italy, the one by Ariminum and Ancona, the other through Etruria.

Hannibal remained undisputed master of Cisalpine Gaul; but the season and his want of siege artillery did not admit of his besieging the posts of Placentia and Cremona, which were still held by Roman garrisons.† He was very desirous to relieve the Gauls from the burthens imposed on them by the presence of his army, and knowing that his first step upon the Roman territory would convert them from doubtful and impatient hosts, into active and zealous allies thirsting for the rich plunder of Italy, he attempted to lead his army across the Apennines into Etruria, but was met by so violent a storm, and his troops suffered so dreadfully from the cold, that he was compelled to return to winter in Gaul. Polybius relates how Hannibal, distrusting the innate treachery and fickleness of the inhabitants, had recourse to various disguises which he changed

* See Observation 1.   † See Observation 2.

frequently during the winter to baffle the attempts he suspected might be made against his life by some Gaulish assassin.

Meanwhile the new Roman consuls chosen for the year 217 were, —

Servilius, who belonged to the aristocratic party, and Flaminius, who, although himself of a patrician family, had procured the passage of an agrarian law, and was on that account very unacceptable to the aristocracy.

A few words may properly be devoted to the character of Flaminius, because we cannot rightly appreciate the greatness of Hannibal without estimating at their real worth the character and abilities of those generals whom he overcame.

Flaminius has been described as a violent wrongheaded man, listening to no counsel, presumptuous and ignorant to excess. But this is the picture drawn by his enemies the Roman aristocracy, who hated him because he espoused the cause of the oppressed and opposed the interests of the moneyed class.

A greater man, the late General Sir Charles Napier, was painted in much the same colours and from the same motives by a powerful moneyed aristocratic Company—whose misgovernment he exposed, and whose favour he disdained to conciliate.

Flaminius was a remarkable man, far in advance of his time, of high principle, and of great public virtue. Seventeen years before the period of which we now speak he was chosen one of the tribunes of the people, and in that capacity carried an agrarian law for the

equal distribution of lands conquered from the Gauls
near Ariminum.   Ten years later he was elected consul
to command against the Gauls; and, after he had assumed his new functions, the Senate, fearing that he
would propose a similar division of any lands he might
then conquer, so worked on the superstitious fears of the
people by the publication of terrible omens and pro-
digies as to procure his recall.   Flaminius received the
despatch ordering him back to Rome when on the eve
of fighting a battle; but, guessing its import, he, in the
spirit of Nelson who turned his blind eye to the signal
to retreat, would not open it until after he had gained
a complete victory; when he replied to the Senate that
the gods themselves having solved their scruples and
pronounced in his favour, it was no longer needful for
him to return.

This incident alone stamps Flaminius as no ordinary
man, and as being possessed of some of the very highest
qualities of a general: impetuous indeed he was, over-
confident it may be, and over-vehement, but still a man
of great qualities both civil and military, to conquer
whom was no small glory.

Flaminius now judging by past experience feared
that his political enemies would endeavour to cancel his
appointment by appealing to popular superstition; he
therefore set out for the army he was destined to command even before the commencement of his term of
office.   Religion, although they themselves might not
believe in it, was a powerful engine whose whole
machinery was in the hands of the nobility, who used it
freely by imposing on the ignorance of the vulgar to

the detriment of those whom they feared or hated. But the Roman aristocracy thought the present no fitting time to stir party animosities, and Flaminius was therefore permitted, without hindrance, to assume the command of the army of Etruria in succession to Sempronius.

The other consul, Servilius, succeeded Scipio at Ariminum; while the last-named general went to Spain, with proconsular power, to take the command of his original army and to oppose the progress of the Carthaginian arms in that country.

The forces which were commanded by Flaminius in Etruria, and by Servilius at Ariminum, were respectively reinforced by two newly raised legions; so that the numbers which would be opposed to Hannibal, on either line he might select for his advance into Italy, amounted to about 30,000 men.

Besides these, two legions were employed in Spain, one in Sicily, one in Sardinia, and another at Tarentum; and the total forces which were maintained in the pay of the republic during this year, including Italian allies, amounted to the large number of 110,000 men.

Early in the spring, Hannibal with his army entered Etruria; leaving Lucca on his right, he advanced to the Arno and became entangled in the marshes of that river, where the sufferings of his troops were extreme, and where it is said that he himself lost the sight of one of his eyes, from the effects of hardship and exposure. Turning to his left, he at length reached firm ground near Fæsulæ, where his soldiers were repaid for their privations by the rich plunder of the valley of the Upper Arno.

Flaminius, who had entrenched himself at Arretium, remained quietly in his camp, and was satisfied with sending to inform his colleague at Ariminum that Hannibal had entered Etruria.*

Hannibal crossed the Arno somewhere in the neighbourhood of Florence : it was a matter of necessity with him to accumulate plunder and to carry it along with his army, no less for the support than for the gratification of his troops; his marches were therefore short, and they were made deliberately past the left flank of the Romans, and almost within sight of their camp, in the hope of provoking Flaminius to follow and attack him.

It was on the impetuous element in the character of Flaminius that Hannibal relied for the success of his plan of operations. He hoped by ravaging the Etruscan territory to draw his enemy after him in hot and angry pursuit, and he was carefully prepared at all moments to turn upon his pursuer, and to take advantage of any error or imprudence into which his eagerness might betray him.

Hannibal, having crossed the Arno, continued his course along its left bank by Aquileia to the Clavis river, thence up the left bank of that river towards Clusium; but instead of approaching Clusium he turned suddenly to the left, crossed the Clavis, and climbing the hills which almost surround the Thrasymene Lake, descended to the north shore of that lake by the road

* See Observation 3.

which leads to Perusia, with the apparent design of ravaging the rich plain of Central Italy which extends from Perusia to Spoletum, and is traversed by the great road from Ariminum to Rome.

Here Hannibal, learning that Flaminius had at length quitted Arretium and was upon his trail, prepared an ambuscade for the Roman army. The ground on the north shore of the lake is peculiarly favourable to such a design. But the uncertainty which prevails as to the exact scene of the battle renders it unprofitable to enter into minute details which can, after all, be little more than imaginary.

The probability is that the battle was fought near the present village of Passignano. At that point, and for some 1500 yards eastward towards Perusia, as well as for 1000 yards westwards, the road runs close to the water's edge on the right, and is hemmed in on the left by cliffs which make it an absolute defile. At the Perusia end of the pass a streamlet falls into the lake from a mountain gorge on the left, and the defile terminates, but the road continues in a straight course over the hills to Perusia. At the end of the defile the lake shore turns to the south-west almost at right angles to the direction of the road, and the hills receding from the lake leave a small plain between them and the water. Here Hannibal placed his heavy Spanish and African infantry to stop the Roman march, while the heavy Gaulish cavalry was to charge the left flank of the advancing column when it emerged from the defile.

All the light infantry was ranged along the top of the

cliffs overlooking the pass, while the Gaulish infantry
and Numidian cavalry, posted in rear of it, were with-

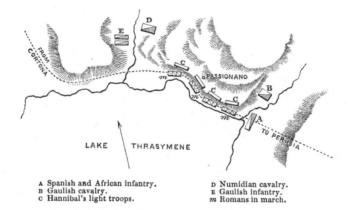

A Spanish and African infantry.   D Numidian cavalry.
B Gaulish cavalry.   E Gaulish infantry.
C Hannibal's light troops.   m Romans in march.

drawn from the road and concealed from sight by inter-
vening high ground.

Flaminius, coming from Cortona, arrived late at night
at the lake shore where he encamped, too late it is said
to examine properly the ground on the line of his next
day's march. He pictured to himself in lively colours
the havoc which perhaps the foreigners were already
making of one of the richest districts of Italy; and
without making any reconnaissance he set forward early
in the morning, eager to overtake the invader. The
morning mist hung thickly over the lake and low
grounds, leaving the heights comparatively clear, and
Flaminius rejoiced in the friendly veil which would
conceal his movements from the enemy's scouts. He
pushed on rapidly, and hoped he might still be in time
to fall on the rear of Hannibal's army while yet in

column of march, and encumbered by the rich plunder of the valley of the Arno.

It is supposed that the head of the Roman column, pressing eagerly forward and suspecting no danger, was attacked in front by Hannibal's infantry, and on the left flank by his cavalry, as it emerged from the Perusia end of the pass; while the Roman main body, still committed in the defile, was overwhelmed by huge stones rolled down from above, and charged by the Gaulish infantry and Numidian cavalry in the rear.

Of the Roman army only 6000 men cut their way through their opponents and escaped off the field to Perusia. Of the remainder, 9000 were made prisoners, the rest were slain; and among the latter was Flaminius himself. In the words of Arnold, " He died bravely, sword in hand, having committed no greater military error than many an impetuous soldier, whose death in his country's cause has been felt to throw a veil over his rashness, and whose memory is pitied and honoured. The party feelings which have so coloured the language of the ancient writers respecting him need not be shared by a modern historian. Flaminius was indeed an unequal antagonist to Hannibal; but in his previous life, as consul and as censor, he had served his country well : and if the defile of Thrasymenus witnessed his rashness, it also contains his honourable grave."

The 6000 fugitives invested in Perusia, destitute of provisions and cut off from all hope of succour, surrendered at discretion. Hannibal retained such of his prisoners as were Roman citizens or of the Latin name; but he allowed the remainder to depart, with the assurance that, far from being their enemy, he had invaded Italy for the purpose of liberating its oppressed peoples from the tyranny of Roman dominion.

The road to Rome now seemed open to the conqueror, whose loss in the late battle was only 1500 men. The army of Servilius was still at Ariminum, and no regular force existed between Hannibal and Rome. But he knew he could not hope to subdue that city so long as she was surrounded by faithful allies.* He must first detach the neighbouring provinces from their allegiance; and the only way to do so was to make their inhabitants personal witnesses of the frequent defeat of the Roman armies, and personal sufferers by the calamities of war, from which they might think they could only escape by deserting the cause of a city which was apparently already deserted by fortune. Hannibal therefore, after ravaging the rich plains of Umbria, and having failed in an attempt to surprise Spoletum, crossed the Apennines in the direction of Ancona, invaded Picenum, and, levying contributions in every direction, marched by the coast-road into Apulia, where he hoped to form for himself a secure base of operations which should be in communication with Carthage by sea.

The Roman spirit rose with disaster; the word "Peace" was not even whispered in the city, nor was it proposed to recall a single soldier from Spain. To remedy the evils of divided command, Fabius was appointed dictator and Minucius his master of the horse or lieutenant.

* See Observation 4.

Quintus Fabius Maximus, chosen dictator in this emergency, belonged to one of the noblest and at the same time most moderate families of the aristocracy, and he was himself of a nature no less gentle than wise. Although probably not a strong believer in the religion of the state, he was a consistent observer of its rites and obligations; because he was convinced that without a reverence for the gods the character of a nation must assuredly degenerate, and that a false religion was therefore far better for its professors than none at all. He knew also what a powerful engine religion or superstition was to influence the masses ; and therefore, on the very day of his inauguration as dictator, he summoned the senate, and, dwelling on the importance of propitiating the gods, moved that the Sibylline books should forthwith be consulted: and, having observed the directions of the oracle, he now turned to oppose the invader.

In anticipation of Hannibal's advance upon Rome, stringent orders were issued to the inhabitants of the districts through which he might be expected to march, to destroy the corn, to burn the houses, to lay waste the lands, and to remove themselves and families and cattle into fortified towns. Bridges were everywhere broken down, and the defences of the city were strengthened.

Meanwhile the army of Servilius was withdrawn from Ariminum and reinforced by two newly raised legions. Of this force, numbering about 50,000 men, Fabius now took the command, and having led it through Campania and Samnium into Apulia, he encamped at the distance of six miles from the Carthaginian army.

The consul Servilius was appointed to command the

Roman fleet and to oppose the Carthaginians at sea, who had just intercepted some reinforcements destined for Spain.

The Romans had now the advantage of general numbers, although very inferior to Hannibal both in number and description of cavalry; they were likewise regularly and plentifully provisioned, and had no occasion to scatter their forces to obtain subsistence, as Hannibal was obliged to do. This last was an immense advantage, for the details of feeding an army require far more study and forethought on the part of a general than the mere fighting.

Fabius kept his army well in hand, following Hannibal when he moved, at a safe distance, and cutting off his foraging parties; being careful always to encamp on ground where cavalry could not act with advantage: so that at length Hannibal, unable to provoke his cautious antagonist to a battle, and disappointed in the hope he had entertained of being joined by the Apulians, once more crossed the Apennines and entered Samnium, where, finding the gates of Beneventum shut against him, he wasted the neighbouring lands and took possession of Telesia; thence descending the Calor to its junction with the Vulturnus, and ascending the latter river till he found a convenient spot, he crossed it near Allifæ, and passing over the hills which separate Samnium from Campania descended by Cales into the Falernian plain.

This district, the richest in Italy, promised an immense booty. Hannibal hoped by his move into Campania either to oblige Fabius to risk a battle to protect it; or, should the dictator continue to avoid an engage-

ment, to induce some of its cities to espouse the Carthaginian cause by furnishing them with so plain a confes-
sion on the part of the Romans of their inability to
protect their allies.

Fabius steadily followed Hannibal, never descending
into the plain, but watching him from the hills.   Again
the Numidian marauders were seen scouring the country
in every direction, and the smoke of burning houses
marked their track.   The Roman soldiers beheld the
sight with the greatest impatience; they were burning
to attack, and Minucius, the master of the horse, encouraged the feeling.   The character of Minucius was
fiery and impatient; he could not tolerate the prudent
policy of Fabius, blamed his incapacity or timidity, and
constantly urged him to attack Hannibal and by one
great stroke to terminate the war.   We may be sure
likewise that, as in modern armies, there was no lack of
self-sufficient young gentlemen (and old gentlemen too,
for that matter) to echo the sentiments of Minucius,
and to criticise freely, and probably with plentiful ignorance, the measures of their general.   But in the words
of Sir Walter Raleigh, " All stirred not this well-advised
commander; for wise men are no more moved with such
noise, than with wind bruised out of a bladder." *

Fabius now conceived the design of enclosing Hannibal in a net.   The Campanian plain, which the Carthaginians were plundering, was enclosed on the south by
the Vulturnus river, over which the only bridge was at
Casilinum and was defended by the Roman garrison of
that town; on the east, the hills from Casilinum to Cales

* See Observation 5.

formed an unbroken barrier, steep and wooded, with very few passes, and these strongly guarded by the Romans; Cales, on the north, was a Latin colony which closed the outlet by the Latin road; and a passage by the Appian road was shut up by several fortified places, and particularly by the difficult and strongly guarded pass of Terracina.

The Roman main body encamped on the hills between Casilinum and Cales, whence all the movements of the enemy could be easily observed.

With all the resources of Samnium in his rear, and on his right in communication with Rome by the Latin colonies of Cales, Casinum, and Fregellæ, Fabius designed to wait patiently until Hannibal's army, having consumed its supplies and possessing not a single town or magazine in Campania, must either starve or endeavour to break its net, and this at such a disadvantage as would, he hoped, insure a defeat which would in Hannibal's position have been total ruin.

Hannibal was aware of the difficulty of wintering in Campania, and had no intention of doing so. He had carefully husbanded his plunder, and he desired now to store it in some safe place, and to get his troops under cover for the ensuing winter in some district which was as yet untouched by the ravages of war. The greatest difficulty against which this great man had to contend, was the necessity of encumbering his movements with the accumulated plunder of Italy, both as a precaution against want and to gratify his soldiers. And, in judging of Hannibal's genius, this great difference between his circumstances and those of his opponents must not be lost sight of; for it was as though a horse weighted with bags of lead ran against another unencumbered, and yet won the race.

Of the two outlets from the Campanian plain by the Appian and Latin roads which led to Rome, neither could safely be attempted by Hannibal, because the Roman army would have followed in his rear, and would have attacked him while endeavouring to force the obstacles in his front.

The same objection applied to his crossing the Vulturnus; for the only bridge over that river was in possession of the Roman garrison of Casilinum, and the passage of so deep and rapid a stream elsewhere could not possibly be safely effected in the presence of the Roman army.

The part of the line offering the best chance of success was that which to a non-military judge appeared the most difficult, viz. the mountains between Cales and the Vulturnus, the passes over which were few, difficult, and strongly guarded. Hannibal designed by a stratagem to entice the Roman troops to quit the passes they were left to guard, and he accomplished his object in the following manner.

Among the plunder were many thousand cattle; and having caused 2000 of the stoutest oxen to be selected, and pieces of split pine or vine branches to be fastened to their horns, these were shortly before midnight driven by the light troops straight to the hills, avoiding the passes guarded by the enemy. The torches about the heads of the poor animals having been previously lighted, the oxen maddened by fear and pain, scattered in all directions over the summit of the hills, and presented to the astonished defenders of the passes the appearance of an army moving over the heights. As soon as the light troops had driven the oxen sufficiently far in the direction they wished them to take, they assembled at the point of the hills above the pass Hannibal designed to force, and, by annoying the Roman troops there posted, confirmed them in the belief that Hannibal's army, in despair of forcing the road, was attempting to break out over the mountains. The Roman troops thereupon quitted the pass, and scaled the heights to interrupt or harass the retreating foe.

As soon as Hannibal saw the lights moving on the top of the heights he commenced his march. The African infantry led the way; they were followed by the cavalry; then came the baggage and booty, and the rear was covered by the Spaniards and Gauls. In this order he followed the road to the defile by which he was to get out into the upper valley of the Vulturnus, and, the pass being deserted by its defenders, his march was unopposed.

Meanwhile Fabius with his main body, confounded by the strangeness of the sight, and dreading lest Hannibal was tempting him to his ruin as he had tempted Flaminius, kept close within his camp until morning. Day broke only to show him his own troops, who should have guarded the passes, engaged on the hills above with Hannibal's light infantry; and presently the Spaniards who formed Hannibal's rearguard (his main body having already cleared the defiles) were seen scaling the heights to reinforce their comrades. The Romans were then driven down towards the plain, and the Spaniards and light troops having thoroughly done their work descended the hills on their side and followed their main body.

Hannibal's design was to winter in Apulia, but he knew that he might safely take advantage of the discouragement of his enemies to extend his devastations before the termination of the season. He accordingly mounted the valley of the Vulturnus towards Venafrum, marched from thence into Samnium, crossed the Apennines, and descended by Sulmo into the Pelignian plain which yielded him a rich harvest of plunder: thence retracing his steps into Samnium, he finally returned to the neighbourhood of his old quarters in Apulia.

The summer was now far advanced: Hannibal had overrun the greater part of Italy, and had invariably been successful in his operations against the enemy; but the allegiance of the Italian states to Rome was yet unshaken, and not a single town had opened its gates to the invader.

That patience in waiting for results, without being depressed by disappointment and without being disheartened by delay, which is a conspicuous mark of a great commander, was possessed by Hannibal in an eminent degree. His great experiment had hitherto failed. He knew that his single army without the aid of allies within the country might overrun, but could not conquer, Italy; and six months had apparently brought him no nearer to such aid than he was after his victory at the Trebbia.

Yet Hannibal was not discouraged. Alone in the midst of enemies, his firm heart resolved that the fidelity of the Roman allies, which his victories during the closing year had been unable to shake, should be tried in the ensuing year by successes still more astounding. Meanwhile he chose the richest part of Apulia for his winter quarters, and took by storm the town of Geronium, where he stored his supplies and sheltered his sick; his army occupied an entrenched camp outside the town.

Fabius, notwithstanding his mortifying failure, followed Hannibal into Apulia, and, being still determined to play the same cautious game, encamped on high ground in his neighbourhood. Fabius was soon after summoned to Rome on business connected with his office. He left the command of the army in his absence to Minucius, strongly enjoining that general to continue to observe his system strictly, and not on any account to risk a general battle.

Minucius immediately approached to within five miles of the Carthaginians and then encamped on a hill (A). Hannibal was in the habit of sending out daily two thirds of his force to forage, keeping the remainder under arms to be ready to succour the foragers if attacked or to defend the camp. Aware of the departure of Fabius, he had little doubt of being able to tempt the impatient disposition of Minucius to hazard a general action. He accordingly drew nearer to the Romans, and encamped on a hill (B) about three miles from their camp, and two miles from Geronium. Between the two armies was a hill (C) which Hannibal occupied during the night by 2000 of his light troops; but next day Minucius attacked the height, drove off its defenders, and encamped there with his whole army.

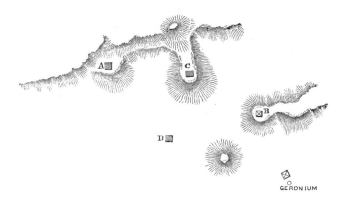

GERONIUM

This approximation of the two armies persuaded Hannibal that a general action, which he so much desired, was at hand, and, in expectation of being attacked by the Romans, he kept his whole force united within his entrenchments. But Minucius on this occasion acted both with skill and judgment: he made no movement; and at length, after vainly waiting for several days, Hannibal, unwilling to consume his provisions and desiring to collect sufficient supplies against the approaching winter, resumed his practice of sending out daily two thirds of his force to forage and to pasture his numerous cattle. Minucius, whose inactivity was designed for the very purpose of inducing his opponent so to act, instantly seized the opportunity afforded by the dispersion of so large a portion of the hostile force, to launch the whole of his cavalry to cut up the

foraging parties, while he marched at the head of his
infantry to assault the weakly defended Carthaginian
camp. Hannibal was too weak to leave the shelter of
his entrenchments, and he had enough to do to defend
his camp against the determined attacks of the Roman
infantry; but he was at length relieved by the arrival of
4000 of his foragers who had sought refuge in the
camp at Geronium, and whom Hasdrubal now led to his
support, and the Romans retired, not however until
they had inflicted considerable loss on their adversaries.*

The day after this check, Hannibal, fearing, from the
ability and boldness shown by Minucius in this affair,
that the Romans might turn the Carthaginian position
in the night and surprise the town of Geronium which
was his depôt, returned to his old camp near that town;
and Minucius immediately occupied the position (B)
which Hannibal vacated.

With the people of Rome, as with our countrymen of
the present day, the only test of military merit was success: the Romans had been previously dissatisfied with
Fabius and impatient of his caution, which they pronounced timidity; and now this success of Minucius,
magnified doubtless by the advocates of a bold policy,
came to increase their discontent with the dictator.
Minucius was raised from the position of a subordinate
to that of a colleague, and his authority was declared
equal to that of Fabius.

This notable measure soon bore the fruit that might

* See Observation 6.

have been expected; for Minucius, elated by his elevation, proposed to Fabius either that they should command the whole army on alternate days, or that each should permanently command one half. Fabius chose the last, because he felt certain that the impetuosity of his colleague would sooner or later get him into trouble with such an adversary as Hannibal, and it was better to risk the destruction of two legions than of four. The Roman force was accordingly divided, and Minucius, withdrawing the troops allotted to him, encamped in the plain at D, at the distance of a mile and a half from Fabius.

Hannibal, apprised of this separation, resolved to play on the lively and impatient disposition of Minucius, and to employ even the success which that general had lately gained to draw him into a snare now. Between Minucius and himself was a hill whose possession might be advantageous to either party; this hill Hannibal designed to seize on ostentatiously, and, by the weakness of the force there stationed, to tempt his adversary to attack it, hoping thus to draw the Romans by degrees into a general engagement, and to defeat them by means of a previously concerted ambush.

The plain which surrounded the hill in question was level, and at first sight did not seem favourable for the concealment of troops, being destitute of wood and of hedges. But Hannibal in a careful examination of the ground had observed several cavities or hollows, some of them capable of concealing several hundred men; and in this broken ground he posted during the night 5000 infantry and 500 cavalry, whose position was such as to enable them to take the Romans in flank and rear, if these last should be tempted to attack the hill in question.

At daybreak on the morrow, Hannibal occupied the hill with his light infantry; and Minucius immediately despatched his light troops supported by cavalry to endeavour to take the height. Hannibal constantly reinforced his Carthaginians by small bodies, and the fight was so obstinately maintained that at length Minucius, whose blood was up, marched towards the hill with his legions in order of battle. Hannibal, on his side, advanced with the remainder of his troops; the battle became fierce and general, and, while at the hottest, he gave the preconcerted signal to his ambush, which charged the Romans in rear and flank. The destruction of the latter appeared certain, and the rout of the Trebbia would have been repeated, had not Fabius, in his anxiety as to the result of the day, held his troops in readiness to support their comrades and led them up at this critical moment to protect the broken legions of Minucius. Fabius now offered battle, but Hannibal, content with his advantage, and unwilling to commit his army against fresh troops, withdrew to his camp.

The Roman loss in this affair was very considerable, and it was so palpable that Fabius had saved his colleague from entire destruction, that Minucius generously acknowledged his obligation, and confessed his inferiority by placing himself once more under the orders of the dictator.

The period of the dictator's office having expired, the two consuls, viz. Servilius, just returned from a successful naval expedition, and Atilius, who was elected on the death of Flaminius, succeeded to the command of the Roman army in Apulia during the interval between the departure of the dictator and the spring elections of the following year.

OBSERVATIONS ON THE PRECEDING CAMPAIGN.

1. The question very naturally suggests itself,—How was it that Hannibal, who was undisputed master of the country, allowed Sempronius and Scipio to quit Placentia, and, after dividing their already small force, to withdraw in safety, the one to Ariminum, the other into Etruria ?

The answer is, that such a movement on the part of the consuls would have been impossible if Hannibal had been on the spot. The relation of these events is obscure ; but we must conclude that the opportunity of his absence at Vicumviæ was taken by the Romans. Hannibal would certainly not have permitted them to draw off their army united, much less in fragments. While the Romans occupied Placentia he was not strong enough to attack them. His attempt on Emporium failed, and he was obliged to find some occupation for his troops, in order by a success elsewhere to remove the moral effect of his failure on the Gauls, on whose fidelity at that time his salvation depended.

2. It may be thought that after the retreat of the consuls from Placentia Hannibal should have laid siege to that place and Cremona, in order to deprive the Romans of their last hold on Cisalpine Gaul. But he could not have besieged those places with any prospect of success, because, 1st, the season was very late and his troops must have suffered severely in siege opera-

tions; 2nd, he was unprovided with the necessary machines or siege artillery, and he does not appear ever to have been properly provided in this respect during his stay in Italy; 3rd, the towns were each defended by 6000 military colonists, who were in fact soldiers; he was conscious that the Roman infantry behind walls was more than a match for his troops; and the mode of fighting, mere bulldog attack and defence, neutralised his own genius which in the open country was worth an army in itself; 4th, he could not afford a failure with such allies as the Gauls.

3. The Roman consuls separated and opposed Hannibal on two different lines of operation, while Hannibal had the choice of either, on which he would have to encounter only one half of the disposable forces of Rome. This was a fatal error, and demands exposure the more urgently because it has been justified by a high military authority*, who has asserted that Servilius was more usefully employed at Ariminum in holding the Gauls in check, than in reinforcing Flaminius. But what had the Romans to fear from the Gauls? Hannibal was the only enemy worth regarding; he alone could render the enmity of the Gauls dangerous to Rome, for he alone could organise and direct it. The whole might of Rome should have been put forth to crush Hannibal himself, —against the man individually; and this the Romans recognised afterwards when they pursued him with such unrelenting hatred to his death. The secret of that hatred was fear. Rome could not feel safe so long

---

* General de Vaudoncourt in his History of Hannibal's Campaigns.

as Hannibal lived, even in exile. One decided success against Hannibal, and the Gauls would have fallen from him like autumn leaves.

Let us now consider how the Roman generals ought to have acted in the position in which they were placed, their object being to cover the rich plains of Umbria, and Rome itself, from the advance of Hannibal.

Flaminius would have done well to remain at Arretium, if he could feel sure that Hannibal would come to attack him in his entrenchments. But the business of the latter was to march towards Rome; that of Flaminius to prevent him. Instead therefore of remaining quietly within his camp and allowing the Carthaginians to turn his flank almost within eyesight, wasting the country in their progress, the moment Flaminius learned that Hannibal had entered Etruria, he should have sent off messengers to Ariminum to concert measures with Servilius for the concentration of the whole Roman force on the line by which Hannibal was about to operate. For this purpose Flaminius should have fallen back to Cortona, and Servilius should have proceeded by forced marches to join him at that place, which covers the approach to the defiles of the Thrasymene lake, and is about seven miles distant from them. But as Hannibal might avoid Cortona and march direct on Clusium, from which place one road led southward to Rome, another eastward, passing south of Lake Thrasymene and by Perusia into Umbria, it was necessary to occupy this important strategical point. Leaving therefore 10,000 men of his force to entrench themselves strongly at Cortona, Flaminius should have

removed his head-quarters with his remaining 20,000
men to Clusium, and, if the Roman scouts were not
worthless, the interior lines which the Romans had to
move upon would enable them to assemble their whole
army at either of those places, or at any point between
them, before Hannibal could reach it.   The above dis-

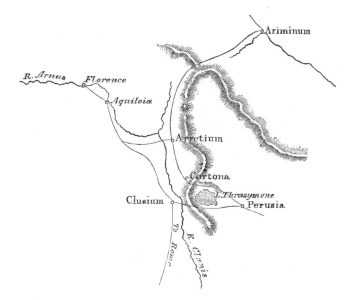

tribution supposes Hannibal to have advanced before
Servilius could arrive at Cortona from Ariminum.   But,
in the case of Servilius having reached Cortona before
Hannibal's approach, the head-quarters of Flaminius
would have been at Clusium, those of Servilius at Cortona; the distance between those places was only fifteen
miles, and the two armies, in constant communication

with each other, would have been able to assemble
60,000 men at the decisive place and time.

On the other hand, if Hannibal had chosen to operate
by Ariminum in place of by Etruria, Flaminius was
well placed at Arretium for moving to reinforce his
colleague on that line.

If either of the consuls had been invested with supreme
command, he might perhaps have ordered the concentration above supposed. But there is no end to the
evils of divided command. It is a saying of Napoleon's,
that "unity of command is the most important thing in
war. Two independent armies should never be placed
on the same theatre."

It may be suggested that Hannibal violated the rules
of war in passing Flaminius, and thereby leaving that
general with 30,000 men on his line of communication.
But Hannibal is not to be judged by common rules.
His whole enterprise was one of life and death ; one
decisive reverse would have been his ruin in whatever
situation he might be ; Hannibal measured the capacity
of his adversary and his own, and acted accordingly.

Yet he never acted rashly, but always with the wisest
calculation and forethought. He would not attack
Flaminius in his camp, but it was his object to destroy
that consul before he could be joined by his colleague.
He never, probably, designed to march into the heart
of Italy leaving 60,000 enemies in his rear, but he
made a show of doing so, and his proceedings were
skilfully based on his knowledge of the character of his
adversary.

It must also be remembered that Hannibal's system

of making war support itself, rendered him to a certain extent independent of communications; he was self-sustaining, and his supplies of all sorts accompanied him; and the quantity of plunder he was thus compelled to carry about added immensely to his difficulties both in marching and fighting.

Although then it may frequently appear in the course of the present narrative that Hannibal violated the arbitrary rules and maxims of war, we shall be sure to find that he did so on profound calculation, and that he gained greatly more by their violation than he would have done by observing them.

Nothing is more certain than that a commander, who is over anxious to square his proceedings by written rules, will never do anything great.

4. It may be asked. Why did not Hannibal march on Rome after Thrasymene?

Because it would have been his ruin.

Rome was defended by the city legions, besides whom every citizen was more or less a soldier, and behind the walls of their own city the Romans would have been invincible. The Carthaginian army, numerically insufficient under any circumstances to undertake such a siege, and destitute of artillery, would have wasted away in a fruitless enterprise, while its provisions were consumed, while its power of procuring fresh supplies was greatly limited by the bitter hostility of the inhabitants, and while the forces of the republic were gathering around it, of which one army of 30,000 men under Servilius was already on its march from Ariminum.

This question will be more fully argued in considering the propriety of marching to Rome after Cannæ.

5. Fabius was a great man and a great general. Why then did he not, with his superior forces, attack Hannibal during this campaign and so end the war by one great stroke?

The answer to the question is, that he did not do so because he *was* a great general. So many reverses had seriously affected the spirit of the Roman troops, and favoured the belief that they were unequal to their enemies in fight. He knew that the opinion and spirit of the soldiers must enter largely into the moral considerations which must influence the decision of a commander as to the adoption of any particular course in war. And Napoleon, in his memoirs, has left us the saying that among those moral considerations one of the most urgent is " the opinion and spirit of the soldier, who is strong and victorious, or feeble and vanquished, according as he believes himself to be either."

The policy of Fabius was gradually to restore confidence by engaging in trifling contests, and only in those where the chances were much in his favour. As Sir Walter Raleigh says in his " History of the World," " he brought them first to look on the lion afar off, that in the end they might sit on his tail."

Another consideration was doubtless Hannibal's great superiority both in number and description of cavalry, which Fabius recognised as having been a principal cause of the Roman reverses, and which now alone enabled Hannibal to keep the field and obtain food for his army.

In determining the plan of a campaign, the relative value of the hostile armies is obviously a most important element to be considered.   And in the determination of that relative value, the relative numbers alone form the least important item.   The reader is referred to the chapter on the " Plan of Campaign," of the " Theory of War," and particularly to the pages 59, 60, and 61, of that chapter, for illustration of the above remarks.   It will be seen thereby that Napoleon considered the personal character of the general as forming the most important item in the determination of the relative value of two armies.

Fabius formed his plan of campaign on a correct estimate of that relative value, and on a careful consideration of the other conditions set forth in the chapter above referred to.   He possessed in the highest degree, one of the most important qualities of a general, viz. calm self-confidence to disregard the impertinence of self-elected advisers, and the murmurings of brave troops impatient to be led to battle.

No amount of disapprobation of his general's plans can justify an officer in canvassing those plans with others, and openly finding fault with them.   Such a proceeding can be productive of no advantage, but on the contrary it is positively injurious.

Unfortunately this word of precept is by no means inapplicable to the officers of our army.   Many young gentlemen set up for generals, and habitually ridicule the dispositions of their superiors.   Such a practice is insubordinate and mischievous in the highest degree; the soldiers acquire the habit from those whose duty it is to set an example; they lose that confidence in their general which is the surest guarantee of success in military operations, and infinite mischief results.

Officers should by all means *study* every order and every movement, but if they disapprove let them do so in secret; the chances are not small that the general is a better judge than they of what is fitting; for he must be acquainted with many facts of which they are ignorant, without the knowledge of which no correct judgment can be formed.

6. Minucius in his attack on Hannibal's camp acted like a bold and skilful soldier; but he appears to have made one great oversight and to have lost an opportunity of straitening his adversary which might never recur.

The magazines on which Hannibal depended for his winter subsistence were in the town of Geronium. If Minucius had directed his cavalry and light troops to march rapidly on that town while he masked the movement by his attack on the Carthaginian camp, they might have burnt the stores there collected, before Hannibal's scattered foragers could rally to defend them.

It was evidently the fear of such a coup that induced Hannibal to fall back on Geronium the day after the attack on his camp.

CHAP. III.

In the spring of the year 216, Terentius Varro and Emilius Paulus were chosen consuls.

Emilius was of the aristocratical party and had given proof of military ability three years before, when he commanded as consul in the Illyrian war.

Varro belonged to the popular party, and was consequently hated by the aristocracy who vainly endeavoured to prevent his election. He was described by the historians of the period as a coarse and brutal demagogue, a butcher's son, and as having been himself a butcher's boy; but these writers were all strong partisans of the nobility; and even though their description of him were not open to distrust on that account, the offices to which he was elected, both before this period and even after his disastrous defeat at Cannæ, as well as his own conduct after that battle, prove that he was an able man and that he possessed some great qualities.

One prætor, Marcellus, who had slain the Gaulish king with his own hand in the last Gaulish war, was at Ostia with one legion. He was destined to command the fleet and to guard the south coast of Italy.

Another prætor, L. Postumius, with one legion, was to watch the frontier of Cisalpine Gaul.

On the arrival of spring the Roman army was still in the neighbourhood of Geronium, and Hannibal in his entrenched camp covering that town. His genius for command had been signally displayed during the winter in governing the heterogeneous materials of which his army was composed. Gauls, the most uncertain and fickle race in the world; Spaniards, the natives of a newly conquered country; and Africans, themselves alien subjects to Carthage, and harshly governed; all remained contented and submissive under his sway during the long inactivity of winter-quarters, which is proverbially trying to the best disciplined troops.

The spring advanced, and Hannibal's supplies were nearly exhausted; the neighbouring country, completely ruined by the presence of the two armies, could no longer furnish provisions. It became therefore necessary to shift his position to provide for the sustenance of his soldiers. Hannibal's circumstances now urgently required that he should gain some signal success, both to encourage his own troops and to intimidate the Roman allies. The great advantage the Romans had over him, consisted in the large magazines of provisions and munitions of war they had formed in various places, which dispensed them from the necessity of scattering their force to seek supplies, and enabled them always to remain united and ready to fall upon the detachments which Hannibal was compelled to make to enable his army to exist. This was the greatest danger to which he was exposed, and was one which, so long as he himself did not possess some towns wherein to store his provisions, it was impossible to remove.

The great Roman magazine of Apulia was at Cannæ, a town near the river Aufidus; and Hannibal suddenly descending into the plains, turned the Roman position and reaching Cannæ by forced marches, captured that town with all its accumulated stores.* He thus not only obtained possession of his enemy's supplies, but interposed between the Romans and the low district of Southern Apulia, where alone at this early season the corn was fully ripe.

By this move the Romans were reduced to choose one of the three following courses, viz. —

1st. To retire and leave Hannibal undisputed master of Apulia.

2nd. To remain in the neighbourhood of Hannibal, but avoiding a battle in continuance of the Fabian policy which would compel them to draw their supplies from a great distance.

3rd. To fight a battle for the recovery of their magazines.

The newly elected consuls now assumed the command of the Roman army in Apulia which was increased by the addition of new levies to eight legions complete, so that the force which was immediately opposed to Hannibal in this memorable campaign amounted to 80,000 infantry and 7200 cavalry.

The army of Hannibal consisted of 40,000 infantry and of 10,000 excellent trained cavalry of whom 2000 were Numidians. His inferiority to the Romans in

* See Observation 1.

actual numbers was very great, but a large proportion of the latter were raw troops, while those of Hannibal were for the most part veterans; and above all he had on his side the immense advantage of a divided command in the army opposed to him, which he well knew was of itself sufficient to balance the disparity of force.

Of the three courses presented to the choice of the Romans, as above stated, the first was not to be thought of for one moment; because the Apulians, already impatient of the burthen imposed on them by the ravages of the Carthaginians, would certainly declare for the invader if the Romans by retiring confessed their inability to oppose him.

The same reasoning, though in a less degree, applied to the adoption of the second course; besides which the difficulty of feeding so large a force from a distance for any length of time, would have been nearly insuperable.

The Roman government, actuated by the above considerations, determined to adopt the third alternative, and sent orders to the consuls to fight a general action. They accordingly broke up from Geronium and approached Hannibal who occupied an entrenched camp in the immediate neighbourhood of Cannæ, at A (see diagram.)

On the second day the Romans encamped at a distance of six miles from the Carthaginians. Here a difference of opinion, as might easily have been foreseen, arose between the consuls, who commanded the Roman army on alternate days. Varro wished to march against

the enemy without delay, while Emilius was averse to
risk an engagement in a country which, being level and
open, was favourable to the action of Hannibal's superior
cavalry.

On the following day Varro, whose turn it was to
command, marched towards the hostile camp. Hannibal attacked the Roman advanced guard on the march
with his cavalry and light infantry; but the Romans
had a decided advantage in the engagement which
lasted for several hours, principally, it is said, owing to
the fact that Varro remedied the inferiority of his
cavalry by the support of a strong body of his heavy
armed infantry, besides that of his light troops.

The same evening the Roman army encamped at B
(see diagram) about three miles from Cannæ, on the
right bank of the Aufidus.

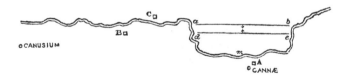

Next morning Emilius, who commanded on that day,
detached one-third of his force across the river to encamp at c, for the purpose of supporting the Roman
foraging parties on that side and of interrupting those
of the enemy.

Two days afterwards Hannibal quitted his camp, and
formed his army in order of battle to tempt the Romans
to attack; but Emilius, sensible that the nature of the
ground was against him, would not move, contenting

himself with strengthening his camps and with the establishment of outposts.

Hannibal, after waiting for some time in his position, at length returned to his camp, whence he detached his Numidians to the other side of the Aufidus to cut off the Roman foraging parties, and to prevent the troops in the small camp on that side from getting water, which at this particular season was an almost intolerable hardship. On the next morning Hannibal, who always made it his particular business to acquaint himself with the characters of his opponents, knowing that Varro was in command, and feeling sure that he was burning with impatience to avenge the insult of the previous day, led his army over the river, and formed it in order of battle, having previously left 8000 men to guard his camp. He probably effected this change of position because the ground on the left bank of the Aufidus presented a wider plain for the action of his cavalry, and because he thought that the surest way to induce the Romans to engage was to threaten their camp on that side.

The situation of the field of battle is a disputed point. Some writers have placed it on one bank of the river, some on the other. But Swinburne tells us that "immediately opposite to the Carthaginian camp, and exactly in that part of the plain where we know with moral certainty that the main effort of the battle lay, the Aufidus, after running due east for some time, makes a sudden turn to the south and describes a very large semicircle." Niebuhr is of opinion that Hannibal formed his army in the loop between *d* and *e;* and after carefully weighing the different accounts this appears on the whole the most probable, provided the chord $d\ e$ be of sufficient length to admit of the formation of such an army as Hannibal's in that space, viz. at least two miles. It may be concluded that so careful an historian as Niebuhr would satisfy himself before giving a decided opinion that the loop of the river was sufficiently large to admit of the formation of the Carthaginian army within it. Let it be assumed then that Hannibal's line of battle extended from d to e. This position protected both his flanks, and thus the numerical superiority of the Romans, so far as related to their power of outflanking him, was rendered unavailing.*

Varro, when he became aware of Hannibal's movement, believing probably that the latter was about to attack the small Roman camp at c, now left 10,000 men in his own camp with orders to march out and attack that of Hannibal during the engagement, and led the rest of his troops over the river, to which having united the troops in the small camp, he then marched left in front and formed his line opposite the Carthaginians in $a\ b$ (see diagram). In the formation of his troops Varro diminished the front and increased the depth of his maniples, by ranging them ten in front and sixteen deep, instead of in sixteen files and only ten deep, which was the usual formation. In making this change he was actuated probably by the belief that he would thereby bring every man of his force to act against the enemy; whereas, if the Romans were disposed in the usual order

* See Observation 2.

the flanks of their army would stretch to a considerable distance beyond the points a and b, and it is evident that all beyond those points would be thrown out of the action.

Hannibal's disposition was as follows. On his left flank, between the infantry and the river, he placed his heavy African and Gaulish horse, 8000 strong. The Numidians, numbering 2000 horsemen, were posted between the infantry and the river on the right flank.* The Spaniards and Gauls occupied the centre of the line of infantry; the Africans, his best troops, whom he had armed after the Roman fashion, were divided between the wings and adjoined the cavalry on both flanks. The infantry was formed in the Grecian method, in double battalions of 1024 men each double battalion, as described in the introductory account of the organisation of the Greek army. The African infantry was as usual in sixteen ranks. But in order to fill up properly the space d e, the Spaniards and Gauls were drawn up in only ten ranks. Thus the Romans diminished, and the Carthaginians increased, their front in the same proportion.

Hannibal commanded the centre in person. Hanno, the right wing. Hasdrubal the left wing. Maharbal commanded the cavalry.

The Roman infantry was formed as usual in three lines, hastati, principes, and triarii. The maniples stood with intervals between them equal to the front of a maniple, and those of the second and third lines covered the intervals of the line in front, so that when

* See Observation 3.

the shock of battle came, the maniples of the second line might move forward to fill the intervals of the first.

The Roman cavalry, properly so called because composed of Roman citizens, numbering only 2400 men, was on the right wing, and was thus opposed to Hannibal's heavy cavalry, 8000 strong: the cavalry of the Italian allies, to the number of 4800 men, was on the left wing, opposed to the Numidians. Emilius commanded the Roman right wing; Varro, the left wing.

The Carthaginians faced the north, so that the wind which blew strong from the south but without a drop of rain, swept clouds of dust over their backs and full into the faces of the enemy.

The battle was commenced by the light troops on both sides, who fought for a long time with equal courage and varying fortune. While they were engaged Hannibal threw forward the centre of his line in the form of a salient angle, which was accomplished by a double direct echellon from the centre—the two centre double battalions and those on their flanks respectively advancing in direct echellon, the right wing from the left, the left wing from the right. This manœuvre was only executed by the Gauls and Spaniards, the African infantry on either flank preserving its original line. In the diagram *a b* and *d e* represent the line of African infantry; *b c d* represents the formation assumed by the Spaniards and Gauls.*

---

* The diagram does not profess to give the proper number of double battalions.

There were in fact about sixteen of these African double battalions, eight on each flank, which stood firm; and sixteen of Spaniards and

While the above formation was in progress, and while the light troops were still engaged, Hannibal ordered

the 8000 heavy cavalry of his left wing to charge the 2400 Roman horse opposed to them; and the latter were immediately defeated and driven from the field by the superior force of the Carthaginians. Emilius, who charged at the head of the Roman cavalry, was severely wounded, but escaped from the slaughter to place himself at the head of the infantry by whose courage he yet hoped to win the day.

Meanwhile the Numidians had orders to amuse the superior allied cavalry opposed to them by demonstrations, but not to allow it to come to close quarters. This they fulfilled ably, and thereby gave time to Hannibal's victorious heavy cavalry to wheel round the rear of the Roman army, and to fall upon the Roman allied cavalry in rear, while the Numidians attacked it in front. The consequence was that not a Roman cavalry soldier alive and unwounded remained on the field.

The combat of the light troops having ceased, they retired through the intervals of their respective lines and formed up, the Romans in the third line with the

Gauls which formed the salient angle. The distance *m c* too is exaggerated; Hannibal's front must have extended about two miles, and *m c* was probably not more than three hundred yards.

triarii, the Carthaginians in a second line behind their first.

The Roman infantry now advanced to the charge, and from the nature of Hannibal's formation the Roman centre first came in contact with the head of the Carthaginian echellon. The shock was great and the fight obstinate, the second Roman line was incorporated with the first, and even the triarii in their eagerness to press forward got mixed up with those in their front.

Hannibal's centre was forced to give way, the salient angle assumed gradually a flatter and flatter shape until it became re-entering. The whole Roman army insensibly crowded towards the gap in the centre of the enemy, and the mass became so closely wedged together that only those on the outskirts had room to use their weapons. They still continued however to gain ground in the direction of Hannibal's centre, which continued slowly to fall back; and now the African infantry on the right and left wheeled inwards and, in perfect order, charged the unwieldy and helpless mass of struggling Romans on both flanks, while Hasdrubal, returned with his victorious cavalry from the pursuit of the Roman horse, broke with thundering fury on their rear.

"Then followed a butchery such as has no recorded equal, except the slaughter of the Persians in their camp after the battle of Platæa. Unable to fight or fly, with no quarter asked or given, the Romans and Italians fell before the swords of their enemies, till when the sun set upon the field there were left out of that vast multitude no more than three thousand men alive and unwounded;"* and these were made prisoners.

Both Livy and Polybius state the number of Romans actually killed to have exceeded 40,000 men. Varro, with a handful of cavalry escaped to Venusia; but the other consul Emilius, the proconsul Servilius, the late master of the horse Minucius, two quæstors, twenty-one military tribunes, and eighty senators, were among the slain.

During the battle, the Romans who had been left behind in their large camp attacked that of Hannibal according to their instructions, but without success, and with the loss of 2000 men.

Of the Roman infantry who had fled from the field, 7000 men took refuge in the small camp which was not far from the right of their line of battle; 10,000 made their way across the river to the large camp. About 15,000 spread themselves over the country and took refuge in the neighbouring towns. During the night following the action about 4000 men quitted the camps and in one body made their way to Canusium, and on the next day the troops which remained in both camps surrendered to the conqueror.

Hannibal's loss in the battle barely amounted to 6000 men. It is no wonder that the Carthaginian officers were elated by this unequalled victory. Maharbal, seeing what his cavalry had done, is reported to have said to Hannibal: "Let me advance instantly with the cavalry; do thou follow to support me, and in four days thou shalt sup in the Capitol." But Hannibal knew

* Arnold.

the resources of the great city and the spirit of its
citizens too well to follow such counsel. Rome, it is
true, was plunged in grief, and if the iron courage of
the Roman aristocracy was for one moment unnerved,
in the next their inborn spirit revived with an elastic
rebound, and the word " peace " being prohibited in the
city, all ranks braced themselves to prosecute the war
with renewed energy.*

* See Observation 4.

OBSERVATIONS.

1. The want of common foresight exhibited by the
consuls Servilius and Atilius, in leaving the great depot
of Cannæ at the mercy of a *coup de main*, is incomprehensible. The distance from that place to their camp
near Geronium was, by the shortest route across the
plain, fifty miles; but the Romans could not safely follow Hannibal's march across the plain, because the Carthaginians, at this time, outnumbered them in cavalry
by three to one; and the road round by the foot of the
mountains was nearly seventy miles long. Under these
circumstances they ought clearly to have given Cannæ
such a garrison and such defences as would have rendered its sudden capture impossible.

There is something not easily explained in the uni-
form neglect of the Romans to organise a more numerous and efficient cavalry. It may almost be said without exaggeration that it was his superiority in that arm
which enabled Hannibal to remain in Italy, as without
it his troops must have starved; and to it he was without contradiction mainly indebted for his victories in
the field.

In ancient times cavalry was undoubtedly the arm
whose effect was the most decisive on the issue of a
battle. The missiles hurled by the heavy infantry
being harmless at a greater distance than twenty yards,
the cavalry could safely hover at a little more than that

distance from the infantry, ready to swoop on any spot where confusion or looseness of order became apparent. The march of infantry therefore across a plain in the presence of hostile cavalry became a very tedious and dangerous operation.

The relative strength of infantry has increased in constant proportion to the improvement of firearms; and at the present day the position of those horsemen, who should sit quietly on their saddles within 600 yards of the muzzles of the Enfield or Whitworth rifles, would be decidedly uncomfortable.

2. Niebuhr's judgment as regards the field of battle has been adopted in opposition to that of all other commentators, because,

1st. All agree that the Romans faced the south, sealing the assertion by the statement that they were consequently nearly blinded by clouds of dust carried full into their faces by the south wind which blew (and still blows) in Apulia daily during harvest time, in which season the battle was fought.

Assuming this to be true, it is impossible that the Romans could have formed their line perpendicular to the river with their right flank only resting on it, because the course of the Aufidus being from S.W. to N.E., the south wind would, in such a case, have blown obliquely into the faces of the Carthaginians.

Arnold, the only author who has done so, has endeavoured to reconcile the discrepancy by forming the Romans perpendicular to the river with their left flank resting upon it, in which position the south wind would blow the dust obliquely into their faces. But in at-

tempting to get over this difficulty, he was driven to the
necessity of placing the Romans with their backs to the
sea, and with the Carthaginians directly interposed
between them and the towns of Canusium and Venusia
on which they must retreat if defeated; a most improbable supposition.

2nd. The diminution of the front of the Roman infantry by increasing the depth is incomprehensible,
excepting on the hypothesis that the outflanking of the
enemy was rendered impossible by some natural obstacle;
and the loop $a\,m\,b$ in the diagram exactly agrees with
this hypothesis.

3rd. Such a field of battle exactly suited Hannibal's
circumstances. The ground was favourable both to the
inferiority of his infantry since the Romans could not
outflank him, and to the superiority of his cavalry
since within the loop the ground is a perfect plain.

So favourable indeed was the supposed field of battle
to Hannibal, that it has been here assumed that the
initiative in crossing the river was taken by him rather
than by the Romans, contrary to the opinion of all other
commentators.

All agree that Hannibal derived great advantage
from having the wind in his back: some say that he
took up his position expressly that he might have the
wind in his back; and one writer goes so far as to say
that on the day before the battle he caused the ground
on which he meant to fight to be ploughed up, so
that there might be a great deal of dust which the
harvest wind might blow into the faces of the Romans.

Without accepting the last statement, nothing is

more probable than that Hannibal should have crossed the river in person with his Numidians the day before the battle to reconnoitre the ground, and, finding it so advantageous, that he should have led his army next day over to the northern bank. The Romans might naturally believe that the small camp, which was only insulted on the previous day, was now to be attacked in earnest; and Varro, impatient to fight and destitute of military talent, was just the general to follow the initiative of his great opponent.

It may be objected to this view of the subject that Hannibal would never have taken up a position with the river in his rear; but the fact is that in the harvest season the Aufidus is everywhere fordable at that distance from the sea; and, even supposing it not to have been so, a decisive defeat would in his circumstances have been certain ruin to the Carthaginian cause in Italy, however open his retreat might have been.

3. Hannibal had probably two objects in view in posting such a large proportion of his cavalry on the left flank; viz.:

1st. To insure the speedy overthrow of the Roman cavalry of the right wing, so that his victorious horsemen might influence decisively the other events of the day.

2nd. If the Romans were defeated, he would thereby be enabled to intercept their fugitives, who would naturally make for the camps which lay to the right of their line of battle, and for Canusium which was distant about five miles in the same direction.

In his orders to the cavalry, Hannibal observed the

Maxim No. 19 of the "Theory of War;"* inasmuch as the Numidians on the right, only 2000 strong, held in check 4800 of the enemy's cavalry by demonstrations, and so enabled the 8000 Carthaginian horse on the left to overwhelm the few squadrons there opposed to them.

It is worthy of remark that Maharbal acted the part of a consummate cavalry officer. Not drawn away by the excitement of pursuit too far from the field, he returned after each success to influence decisively the fate of the day; whereas, had he pursued the Roman horse of the right wing off the field of battle, his success would have had no effect on the general issue; the cavalry of one wing of both armies would have been absent, — nothing more. But Maharbal returned to overthrow the Roman cavalry of the left wing also, and leaving them to be pursued by the Numidians, he then made that charge on the rear of the Roman infantry which decided the day. His conduct stands in honourable contrast to that of Rupert at Naseby, of Jean de Vert at Nordlingen, and of too many cavalry commanders; but it must be remembered that the power of a cavalry officer to arrest his troopers while in the headlong pursuit of a flying enemy, depends fully as much on the general discipline of the men as on the will of their officer at the moment. Unless cavalry is always well in hand, the force is well nigh useless; and without previous discipline, the trumpets during a pursuit will sound the recall in vain.

* Page 151, "Theory of War."

The Roman infantry present on the field exceeded 60,000 men, and their formation in such deep masses rendered their very numbers a source of weakness. If 40,000 had been formed in the usual manner, and the remainder been kept in reserve, the result would probably have been very different. The Roman infantry was fully equal to that of Hannibal in a hand to hand fight. The struggle between the two lines would have been doubtful, and if the Africans wheeled inwards (as they actually did), to charge the flanks of the Roman mass, the Roman reserve would have turned the tables, and charged the Africans in flank and rear.

It was a terrible mistake of the Roman general to oppose 2400 of the *élite* of his cavalry to 8000 of the enemy. It would have been better, if he was determined to fight in the plain, to extend his infantry on one flank to the river, in the order best calculated to resist cavalry; to post the 4800 allied horse on the other flank; and to hold his 2400 Roman horsemen in rear with the reserve infantry, ready to reinforce the allied horse, or to act wherever their presence might be most necessary. He could not insure his being superior in cavalry at the decisive point, because the enemy was the stronger in that arm; but he should have acted so as to be *as strong as possible* at that point, and to remedy his inferiority by rapidity of movement and manœuvring.

The 4800 Roman cavalry of the left wing ought to have gained a decided success in that quarter. They should have advanced against the Numidians, charged them if they resisted, and driven them off the field;

then, leaving 1000 to hold the Numidians in check, the remainder should have fallen on the flank and rear of Hannibal's Africans of the right wing, uncovered by the retreat of the cavalry; while the Roman infantry of the left wing, regardless of the fight in the centre, should have charged them in front. Hannibal's right wing must have been defeated before his heavy cavalry could have come to its support, for the line of battle was two miles long. Meanwhile, the centre of Hannibal's line would have been forced back (as it actually was); and it would have been hard if, with such troops as the Romans, their reserve of 20,000 infantry and 2400 cavalry, coming into action at this moment, had not been able to complete the victory even against Hannibal.

4. Most historians and commentators have blamed Hannibal for not marching on Rome the day after Cannæ. Even Napoleon has added his voice to the general condemnation.

If Hannibal was likely to find the citizens in such abject fear and despondency that they would open their gates to him, he may justly be blamed; but is it likely such would have been the case? Even though the Romans had not been a people whose courage and constancy under reverses have never been surpassed, hardly ever equalled, it is well known how great is the courage of despair. The Romans were a much greater people than the Carthaginians, and yet if we consider the example of Carthage, when, denuded of almost all power of resistance, every man, woman, and child united to defend their city to the last, we may estimate the resistance Hannibal might expect to meet with at the gates of Rome.

There was however no cause for despair. Such a movement of Hannibal was the very one his enemies ought to desire. Behind walls, that discipline which is everything in the field is comparatively unnecessary, and natural courage equalises the untrained defender with the veteran assailant. The population of Rome was essentially warlike, and there was no lack of arms. The two city legions formed the regular garrison of the capital, numbering 10,000 men. The levy *en masse* of all above seventeen years of age provided two additional legions and 1000 cavalry. Eight thousand slaves who were willing to serve were enlisted and armed, and, besides these, a number of criminals and debtors were glad to purchase pardon by taking up arms in defence of the State. The prætor Marcellus was at Ostia with 10,000 men about to embark for Sicily. Thus, the force which could have been assembled to oppose Hannibal, four days after the arrival of the news of Cannæ, amounted to—

Two city legions	10,000
Levy *en masse*	11,000
Slaves, prisoners, &c.	12,000
Marcellus from Ostia	10,000
	43,000

Hannibal had 34,000 infantry. The distance from Cannæ to Rome was, for the Carthaginian army encumbered with spoil, at least twelve days' march; and this distance excluded all possibility of a surprise, the hope of which could alone justify his marching upon Rome; for, notwithstanding the boast of Maharbal, his cavalry unsupported could do nothing against the city.

It is not possible that an assault on a city so strong in its walls and in the spirit of its defenders should have succeeded. For a regular siege Hannibal's force was insufficient, and he had no artillery; he was, besides, not partial to sieges, the circumstances of which, to a great extent, neutralised the superiority of his genius. He must have carried with him the supplies he had accumulated for the subsistence of his force, and when they should be consumed he would be destitute. Fresh Roman levies would gather on his rear, and before long his own army would become the besieged. In such an undertaking he would have wasted time, and, above all, that prestige which he had acquired by his late astonishing victory.

The fact that Hannibal did not think himself strong enough to make an attempt on Canusium, defended by only 10,000 dispirited fugitives from Cannæ, is a sufficient answer to those who say he should have besieged Rome. For it was certainly a great mistake, if he could have prevented it, to allow this nucleus for a new army to escape him.

CHAP. IV.

FOURTH AND FIFTH CAMPAIGNS.

GREAT was the mourning in Rome when it was known that another great battle had been lost, another consul slain, and another Roman army destroyed. "Our colder temperaments scarcely enable us to conceive the effect of such tidings on the lively feelings of the people of the South, or to image to ourselves the cries, the tears, the hands uplifted in prayer or clenched in rage, the confused sounds of ten thousand voices giving utterance with breathless rapidity to their feelings of eager interest, of terror, of grief, or of fury." *

The senate, of its own authority, immediately named a dictator, M. Junius, to provide for the safety of the State, who chose Tib. Sempronius Gracchus for his master of the horse. These two officers enrolled all the male population above seventeen years of age for the defence of the city, and by this means obtained two legions and 1000 cavalry in addition to the two city legions which formed the regular garrison. They likewise enlisted 8000 slaves and 4000 debtors or criminals, on promise of freedom and pardon for past offences.

* Arnold.

At length despatches arrived from Varro, which informed the senate that he had rallied the wreck of the army at Canusium, and that Hannibal was not marching upon Rome.

Nearly at the same time, news arrived from Sicily that one Carthaginian fleet was ravaging the coasts of Hiero king of Syracuse, the Roman ally, while another threatened a descent on Lilybæum and the Roman portion of the island, for the purpose of preventing the Roman fleet there stationed from going to the assistance of Hiero. Titus Otacilius, who commanded that fleet, represented to the senate that an additional naval force must be sent, if the possessions of the republic in Sicily were to be retained.

The peril at home was too great to comply with this requisition. Marcellus, who lay at Ostia, with a fleet destined for the above service, was detained. He was ordered to send 1500 of his naval conscripts to reinforce the garrison of Rome, while he himself repaired with his one legion to Canusium, to take over the command of the troops at that place from Varro who was summoned to Rome, and to organise a new army to oppose Hannibal.* The diminished fleet then sailed from Ostia to reinforce Otacilius, under one of the prætors, Marcus Furius.

Meanwhile, such had been the panic among the fugitives from Cannæ, that many young nobles, despairing of the salvation of their country, planned an escape beyond sea with the design of entering some foreign service. The wise and firm intervention of Varro, how-

* See Observation 1.

ever, prevented the execution of a plan which would have been the signal of a general panic;—for what Roman colony or what ally could be expected to make sacrifices in the cause of a city which its noblest citizens themselves deserted as hopeless?—and that consul, after having done this great service, handed over his command to Marcellus, and repaired to Rome in obedience to the orders of the senate.*

Varro had little mercy to hope for at the hands of his countrymen, never indulgent to a defeated general; for if the memory of Flaminius was persecuted, notwithstanding his glorious death, what could he expect, a fugitive general from that field whose disasters were principally owing to his rashness, and where his colleague and nearly all his soldiers had perished? Demosthenes dared not trust himself to the Athenian people after his defeat in Ætolia; but Varro, with a manlier spirit, returned to bear the punishment and disgrace which the general feeling, sharpened by political hatred, was so likely to inflict.

The senate was composed of his bitter political enemies; but that body nobly responded to the confidence he manifested in it. Party feeling was suspended; the political adversary, the defeated general, were alike forgotten; it was only remembered that Varro had resisted the after-panic among his troops, and had submitted himself to the judgment of his countrymen; and the senate thanked him publicly "because he had not despaired of the commonwealth."

In pursuance of his policy to detach the states of

* See Observation 2.

Italy from Rome, Hannibal, after Cannæ, dismissed all his prisoners of the Italian allies without ransom. He was now in want of money, and having informed his Roman prisoners that he would admit them to ransom at so much a head, he allowed a deputation from their body to accompany his ambassador to Rome, in order to treat with their families for the price of their liberation.

The senate however not only refused to discuss any terms of peace with his envoy, as Hannibal had hoped, but absolutely forbade the ransom of any of the prisoners, thinking it neither politic to enrich their adversary with so large a sum as he would obtain thereby, nor to show indulgence to soldiers who had surrendered to the enemy.

Pliny relates that Hannibal, exasperated by this refusal, practised inhuman cruelties towards his captives. But, besides the fact that this is the testimony of an enemy, wanton cruelty formed no part of Hannibal's character, and neither Livy nor Polybius mentions these stories. Such cruelty moreover would have been impolitic in the highest degree, as tending to prevent any Roman soldier for the future from ever surrendering himself alive; and politic sagacity is the quality above all others for which the great Carthaginian is most renowned.

The battle of Cannæ, and Hannibal's behaviour after it, were too much for the fidelity of some of the Roman allies. Apulia declared for the conqueror immediately, and the towns of Arpi and Salapia opened their gates to him. Bruttium, Lucania, and Samnium were ready to follow. Hannibal himself marched into Samnium to take possession of Compsa, which was delivered up to him by the popular party, and having there stored his plunder and heavy baggage, he sent his brother Mago with one division of his army into Bruttium to take possession of such towns as might submit, and to organise the efforts of his partisans in that province.

Hanno, with another division, was sent into Lucania, to act the same part; while Hannibal, with his main body, descended into Campania, and attempted to surprise Neapolis and Cannæ on the coast, the possession of which would have placed him in short and easy communication with Carthage by sea; but finding those places too strongly garrisoned, he marched upon Capua, which concluded an alliance with him, and received the Carthaginian army within its walls.

Meanwhile, Marcellus had withdrawn from Canusium when Hannibal moved towards Compsa, and, marching by the shorter route of Beneventum, took post at Casilinum, between Capua and Rome, to cover the passage of the Vulturnus; while the dictator, M. Junius, with 25,000 men, advanced from Rome and occupied a position at Teanum, about twelve miles in his rear.

Mago now embarked at one of the ports of Bruttium, to carry the news of his brother's success to Carthage, and to demand reinforcements. During the progress of this great struggle, neither Rome nor Carthage could be said to have the mastery of the sea. A constant stream of reinforcements from Africa might have landed in Bruttium, and fortunate was it for Rome at this time that Hannibal's bitterest enemies were to be found, not in Italy, but in the Carthaginian senate, where the intrigues of Hanno and his faction, joined to the demands made on Carthage by the war in Spain, withheld those succours from Italy which might have enabled Hannibal to terminate the struggle by the conquest of Rome.

The accession of Capua was the greatest result, short of the submission of Rome itself, which could have followed from the battle of Cannæ, and the Campanian towns of Calatia, Atella, Acerræ, and Nuceria soon followed its example, by submitting to the conqueror. Nola, about midway between Capua and Niceria, was held by a Roman garrison; but the popular party in that town favoured Hannibal, and Marcellus, having learnt the existence of a plot to deliver it into his hands, marched round from Casilinum by the hills suddenly to Nola, where he overawed the disaffected and repulsed Hannibal in an assault with considerable loss.

The place of Marcellus at Casilinum was to have been filled by the advance of M. Junius from Teanum; but the movements of the latter were too slow, and Hannibal anticipating him, laid siege to Casilinum. The obstinate resistance of the garrison however obliged him to convert the siege into a blockade * ; and, leaving a part of his force to guard his lines of circumvallation, he withdrew the remainder to winter quarters in Capua.†

The dictator remained at Teanum, and Marcellus in a fortified camp on the hills above Nola.

In Cisalpine Gaul, the prætor L. Postumius, early in

---

* See Observation 3.   † See Observation 4.

the following year (215 B.C.), fell into an ambuscade, in which himself was slain, and his army destroyed.*

Meanwhile in Spain, during the year 216 B.C., the two Scipios had defeated two Carthaginian armies under Hanno and Hasdrubal, and driven them beyond the Iberus; and these successes not only cooled the native Spaniards towards the alliance of Carthage, thereby depriving that city of the best nursery of soldiers for the reinforcement of Hannibal, but occupied moreover a large body of African troops which might otherwise have been sent to Italy.

The pressing necessities of Rome prevented any supplies of money being sent during the winter to the Roman forces in Sicily and Sardinia. In Sicily, the friendship of Hiero supplied the deficiency; but in Sardinia contributions were levied on the inhabitants, who applied for assistance to Carthage, and, in the following year, openly revolted against Rome.

Before the end of the winter, the garrison of Casilinum reduced to the last extremity by famine, capitulated, without any vigorous effort appearing to have been made by the Romans to relieve it. But the relation of these operations is confused, and it is impossible to understand how a town, situated as Casilinum was, astride on the Vulturnus, and possessing a bridge, could have been blockaded by Hannibal effectually, as his army must in that case have been cut in two by the river, and the portion on the right bank exposed to destruction from the army of the dictator at Teanum.

* See Observation 5.

However that may be, Hannibal obtained possession of the town; and its important position, covering Capua and commanding a bridge over the Vulturnus, induced him to place there a garrison of 700 of his best troops.

FIFTH CAMPAIGN.

The consuls elected for the year 215 were Fabius Maximus, formerly dictator, and Tiberius Gracchus.

Rome made gigantic efforts to carry on the war, and the forces for the year were distributed as follows :—

	Legions.
Fabius succeeded the late dictator in the command of his army, which moved from Teanum to Cales, and consisted of	2
Tib. Gracchus commanded new levies of volunteer slaves. He took post at Sinuessa on the coast for the purpose of protecting Cumæ and Neapolis, and his force amounted to	2
Marcellus, still in his camp above Nola, continued in command of	2
Marcus Valerius, prætor, commanded in Apulia	2
Appius Claudius, prætor, had in Sicily	2
Qu. Mucius, prætor, in Sardinia	1
The Garrison of Tarentum consisted of	1
Publius Scipio commanded in Spain	2
	14

The army which Postumius lost in Cisalpine Gaul was not replaced; but Varro was sent to Picenum to raise soldiers, and to intercept any Gaulish reinforcements which might attempt to join Hannibal by the coast road.

To meet the extraordinary demands on the treasury for the maintenance of the above force, which, including allies, represented a grand total of 140,000 men, the government had recourse to the simple expedient of doubling the year's taxes; and although the destruction of so many sources of wealth by the war, and particularly the ruin of the agricultural interest, must have caused this measure to press with great severity on the poorer classes, the people were in no mood to refuse any sacrifice however costly, and the money was paid.

Even in the revolted provinces, a guerilla warfare was organised against the Carthaginians and the revolted Italians, from among the peasants and slaves who were employed on the public domains: and most of the principal towns of Southern Italy continued faithful to the Romans, because they had long since converted them into Latin colonies.*

In Apulia, Brundisium on the sea-coast, and Luceria and Venusia inland; in Lucania, the town of Pæstum on the coast; in Samnium, that of Beneventum on the great Appian road,—were so many fortresses held by Latin garrisons in the very heart of the revolted districts; while the Greek cities of Cumæ and Neapolis, in Campania, were held for Rome by their citizens with no less devotion.

We have unfortunately no reliable statement of the

---

* The Latins were to be depended on the same as the Romans themselves. Their connection with Rome was more intimate than that of any other state, and although they did not, of right, enjoy the Roman franchise, they yet possessed many valuable privileges, and hoped to obtain more. All the cities of ancient Latium were long since become Roman, that is to say, colonised by Roman citizens. Unfaithfulness to Rome was thought impossible in her Latin allies; Samnium and Capua might revolt, but the fidelity of the Latin name was not to be shaken.

forces which Hannibal could oppose to the overwhelming numbers of his enemies. His army, after Cannæ, consisted of about 34,000 foot and 9,000 horse. He detached two divisions into Bruttium and Lucania, to organise the insurrection of the inhabitants, and these detachments must have had enough to do to hold their own against the three Roman legions in Apulia (viz. the army of M. Valerius, and the garrison of Tarentum), and to keep down the guerillas. The reinforcements expected from Carthage were inconsiderable, and consisted altogether of cavalry and elephants; but Hannibal's own force must have been greatly augmented by the Samnite levies, and by those which Capua could furnish*, or he could not have kept the field at all. We may therefore conclude that the place of his absent divisions was supplied by his new allies, and that he commanded in person at least 35,000 foot and 10,000 horse.

In other quarters, the prospects of Hannibal were very favourable.

Ambassadors came to him in Campania from Philip king of Macedon, to conclude an alliance offensive and defensive and to arrange the landing of a Macedonian army in Italy.

He was in hopes of obtaining possession of Tarentum, where the popular party had been in correspondence with him ever since the battle of Cannæ, and that town would have been a most important acquisition as afford-

* Livy states that Capua could supply an army of 30,000 foot and 4000 horse.

ing a seaport convenient for communication both with Macedon and Carthage.

Sardinia was in open revolt against Rome; and, in Sicily, Hiero Rome's faithful friend was dead, and his grandson Hieronymus concluded an alliance with Hannibal.

As soon as the season arrived for active operations, Hannibal took post on Mount Tifata above Capua, and there entrenched himself. The several Roman armies commanded by Fabius at Cales, by Gracchus at Liternum to which place he advanced from Sinuessa, and by Marcellus at Nola, amounting in the aggregate to 60,000 men, were all around him.

But Tifata was a strong position; its numerous glades furnished grass in abundance for Hannibal's cattle, and cool and healthy summer quarters for his men;—and Hannibal sat quietly on the summit of his crag to watch the working of the elements he had invoked, and to break forth like the lightning flash when the storm should be fully gathered.

Thus the summer of this year was like the breathing time of two gladiators, each narrowly watching the condition of his adversary, and looking where to plant the next blow. Fabius, resolving to pursue his old cautious policy of harassing the enemy, cutting off his supplies, and avoiding a decisive battle, procured a decree of the senate ordering the inhabitants of the districts which either then were, or were likely to become, the seat of war, to clear their corn off the ground and carry it into the fortified cities before the 1st June, on pain of wasting the lands, burning the buildings, and selling the slaves of all who neglected to comply.

The season was advancing and Gracchus was occupied at Liternum with the drill and discipline of his heterogeneous army, when he received a message from the inhabitants of Cumæ, that the Capuans had invited them to assist at the fête which was celebrated yearly at Hamæ by the several Campanian cities. The Capuans were to send an armed force to protect those engaged in the festivities from interruption by the Romans. The Cumæans had accepted the invitation, but, fearful of treachery, they warned Gracchus of the circumstance. Hamæ was only three miles distant from Cumæ; Gracchus entered the last-named town the night before the intended fête, and, on the following night, he surprised the Capuans, and killed 2,000 of their number.

Hannibal no sooner heard of this disaster, than he marched to Cumæ, and was repulsed in an assault on that place by Gracchus with the loss of 1300 men*, and, after vainly endeavouring to provoke the Romans to a battle in the open country, he returned to Tifata.

Fabius now moved from Cales to effect a junction with Marcellus in a camp which the latter occupied on a hill above Suessula. Casilinum being in the enemy's hands, Fabius was obliged to cross the Vulturnus opposite to Allifæ†, to march down the left bank to its confluence with the Calor where he crossed that stream, and thus by a circuitous march, to join Marcellus. Afterwards being anxious for the safety of Nola, where the popular

---

* See Observation 3, concluding paragraph.

† See Observation 3.

party was again plotting to deliver the town to Hannibal, Fabius sent Marcellus with his army to garrison Nola, while he occupied the camp of Suessula in his stead.

Gracchus on his side advanced from Cumæ towards Capua, so that 60,000 Romans were collected round Hannibal, who would not indeed in the open plain have hesitated to attack them all united, had the Roman generals given the opportunity.

The Roman armies were in free communication with each other, and could easily concentrate before Hannibal could reach either of them, if their generals desired to engage. But such was not their game. If Hannibal marched against either army, it would draw him away to the hills, while the other laid waste the country round about Capua which it was Hannibal's particular object to protect.

Hannibal was in a dilemma; he was unwilling to leave Capua unprotected, yet it was of consequence to encourage his partisans in Nola, by approaching that town, into which it was possible they might be able to give him admission.

Besides this, his long-expected reinforcements of cavalry and elephants had landed in Bruttium, and unless he should make some movement to protect their junction with him, they might be intercepted and destroyed by Fabius from Suessula.

Hannibal therefore abandoned Tifata, and timed his march to Nola so accurately, that he was joined by his reinforcements while before that town, which, in ignorance of the strength of the garrison, and counting on the goodwill of some of the inhabitants, he hoped to take by escalade.* But Marcellus, watchful and bold, defeated an assault with great loss to the Carthaginians by a sudden sally; after which, Hannibal, rendered uneasy by the desertion during the following night of 1200 of his newly arrived troops, and fearing for a further bad effect of his repulse on the spirit of his soldiers, marched into Apulia and fixed his winter quarters near Arpi.†

Gracchus followed him with one consular army and took up his quarters in Luceria, while the other under Fabius remained at Suessula. Marcellus, after retaining a sufficient garrison to secure Nola, was directed to dismiss the rest of his soldiers to their homes.

In Apulia during the winter the troops of Gracchus and those of Hannibal engaged frequently in partial encounters, and it always happened that whenever Hannibal was personally absent, the advantage was on the side of the Romans, who thus became daily better acquainted with their enemies, and acquired greater confidence in themselves.

In Bruttium, during the closing year, the town of Petelia had defied during eight months all the efforts of Himilcar, one of Hannibal's lieutenants, to capture it; and had done good service to Rome by giving full occupation to the Carthaginian troops in that quarter; but its ultimate surrender was followed by the reduction of Consentia, Locri, and Crotona, in rapid succession.

Meanwhile in Spain the two Scipios had, during the year 215 B.C., continued to advance in their career of

---

* See Observation 6.   † See Observation 7.

success, and had defeated the Carthaginian generals in two pitched battles with great loss.

The Roman operations in Sardinia had likewise been completely successful.

In another quarter too fortune favoured the Romans; for the ambassadors of Philip of Macedon were, on their homeward voyage, captured by a Roman fleet and carried prisoners to Rome; thus at once revealing the impending danger, and giving time for the necessary measures to forestall it by attacking Philip at home. For this purpose M. Valerius, prætor, who commanded two legions in Apulia, was ordered to take the command of the Roman fleet at Tarentum and Brundisium, and to cross the Ionian gulf to endeavour to form a Greek coalition, against Macedon, of the Ætolians and other tribes which bordered Philip's western frontier.

Thus, on the whole, the prospects of Rome were decidedly improved; Hannibal had been unable to mark the campaign with a victory, and the Romans, encouraged by the prosperous turn of their affairs, were ready to make even greater sacrifices than had yet been demanded of them for the prosecution of the war.

OBSERVATIONS ON THE FOURTH AND FIFTH CAMPAIGNS.

1. The relation of the events of these two campaigns is very obscure. We are told that Marcellus marched from Ostia with one legion, and that he was allowed by Hannibal to pass within a few miles of his victorious army, and to enter Canusium, there to organise a new force. But this it is impossible to believe. The explanation is probably that Marcellus himself alone repaired to Canusium, to take over the command from Varro.

It appears strange that Hannibal did not march on Canusium and attempt to capture it immediately after Cannæ. It was garrisoned by only 10,000 men, who had just suffered a most depressing defeat, and were many of them without arms. The disorganisation of the garrison is evidenced by the intended desertion of many of the officers, and Hannibal would have been justified in expecting that his appearance before Canusium, on the day after the battle, would be followed by the surrender of the town.

We are in ignorance of Hannibal's reasons; but he left the Roman troops in Canusium to recover from their consternation, and to form the germ of a new army; and the fact of his not being in a condition to undertake the reduction of that place, is a sufficient answer to those who find fault with him for not marching against Rome.

Yet, although he may not have been able to reduce Canusium, he was able to prevent a body of 10,000 men under Marcellus from entering it almost under his nose. But we may have sufficient faith in the genius of Hannibal to feel sure that he did not commit such an oversight, and that our perplexity in this instance, as in others, arises from the loose and disjointed manner in which the historians of the period have chronicled the events of the war.

2. The conduct of Varro at Canusium, in resisting the panic among his troops, and his manly submission to the will of his country, prove that, although ignorant of war, he was possessed of qualities which are very valuable in a commander. As a citizen he must have been a very remarkable man, as is shown by the estimation in which he was held even by his political enemies notwithstanding the disaster of Cannæ, so that some writers relate that he was offered the dictatorship immediately thereafter by the general voice of the senate and people, but that he refused to accept the office. And although the truth of this story is more than doubtful, the fact of its having been believed at all is a proof of the general respect in which he was held.

It is certain that Varro continued to exercise authority as consul after the battle of Cannæ, during the remainder of the year; for he is spoken of by the best historians as commanding a legion in Apulia after Marcellus withdrew from Canusium, although the fact has not been noticed in this narrative, because it is not told anywhere when he went, how he went, or how his legion was raised. In the succeeding year Varro was employed as proconsul, and we find him constantly in authority to the very end of the war.

The above facts ought to be sufficient to overbear the testimony against him of writers who were his political enemies.

3. It is difficult to account for the apathy with which the armies of Junius Gracchus and Marcellus witnessed the blockade and surrender of so important a place as Casilinum, which in Roman hands would be a constant thorn in the side to Capua at the distance of only three miles; and was moreover a most important strategical point, covering the road to Rome and commanding the only bridge over the Vulturnus. The proper position for Junius and his army was at Casilinum, not Teanum.

But the whole account of the capture of Casilinum by Hannibal is irreconcilable with what we know to have been its situation. Livy tells us that the town was divided by the Vulturnus into two parts, and that a permanent bridge afforded communication between them. How then could Hannibal blockade the town? To do so he must pass half of his army to the right bank of the river, which would thus be separated from the other half by a deep and rapid stream, not fordable; and these separated halves would be exposed to be attacked on the one side by M. Junius from Teanum, on the other by Marcellus from Nola, to say nothing of the difficulty of effecting the passage of such a river in the face of the army of the dictator, which would naturally approach Casilinum from Teanum, directly such an operation should be threatened.

The possession of Casilinum conferred greatly the

advantage of "interior lines" on the party holding that place. When Fabius, in the campaign of 215, wished to effect a junction with Marcellus, he could not do so without undertaking a long and arduous march round by Allifæ, by which he uncovered Rome. If Hannibal had desired to advance on that city, the possession of Casilinum enabled him to cross the Vulturnus at that place, and thereby to gain a long start of his enemies.

So important is the strategical position of Casilinum, that it has now become a strong fortress under the name of Modern Capua.

If Casilinum had been maintained, Hannibal's march to Cumæ in the campaign of 215 would have been full of risk. The army of Fabius would have been at Casilinum, and might have followed the Carthaginian march to Cumæ, not close enough to be forced to an action by Hannibal suddenly turning upon it, but ready to attack the enemy in rear while Gracchus sallied from the town upon his front.

4. Nearly all the historians of Hannibal have followed the example of Livy in blaming him for exposing his army to the temptations and luxuries of Capua, and in attributing to the consequent demoralisation of his troops, the undoubted fact that from the winter there spent dates the change in the fortunes of the great Carthaginian.

But these reproaches are destitute of all just foundation. Hannibal's troops did not, after that winter, manifest any falling off in discipline or courage; but the Roman armies from this time forth were led by generals who estimated correctly the personal superiority of their great antagonist, who gave him no opportunity to strike any more of his deadly blows, but reduced him to wage a petty warfare of small posts, or of sieges in which the lustre of his genius always appeared to disadvantage, and in which his strongest arm, the cavalry, was comparatively useless.

This was the real reason why so powerful a confederacy of Italian States against Rome, supported by an army of 30,000 veteran and victorious soldiers, and the whole directed by a general who has never been surpassed,—was only formed to be defeated. This was the reason why the revolt of Capua was the term of Hannibal's progress; why from this time forward his genius was shown rather in repelling defeat than in commanding victory; why, instead of besieging Rome, he was soon employed in protecting Capua; and why his protection was finally unavailing.

5. Notwithstanding the success of the Cisalpine Gauls against Postumius, no hostile movement against Rome was made from Gaul; and it appears strange that some experienced Carthaginian officer was not sent to organise and direct the Gaulish insurgents, and to endeavour to induce the Etruscans and Umbrians to join the Southern confederacy against Rome, which was directed by Hannibal.

6. Hannibal's intelligence appears to have been defective. On two different occasions he attempted to take Nola by a *coup de main*. He would hardly have done so had he known that the town was defended by a consular army of 20,000 men; and he could not hope to

carry on a regular siege while the Romans had so strong
a force at hand to interrupt it.

7. After his last unsuccessful attempt on Nola, Hannibal quitted Campania to winter in Apulia. This
proceeding has the appearance of leaving Capua to the
mercy of the Roman armies. But Capua was the
second city of Italy, capable it is said of maintaining a
force of 34,000 men. Its garrison and its walls were
therefore strong enough to defy all enemies save one,
viz. famine; and Hannibal's object in quitting Campania
was to husband the resources and magazines of Capua,
which must otherwise have been expended in feeding
his army during the winter. He remained in the
neighbourhood long enough to enable the Capuans to
gather in the harvest of the year unmolested by the
Romans, and that object being effected he was better
elsewhere.

Although we are not told that such was the case,
Hannibal must have previously formed a large magazine
of provisions at Arpi, where he wintered.

During this campaign, Capua was Hannibal's pivot of
operations. At one period there were actually around
him, including the force of Valerius in Apulia, eight
Roman legions. It was in such a situation that this
great man displayed all the resources of his genius.
His ascendancy was so great that his enemies never
dared to take the initiative in attacking him; but, on
the contrary, from his watch-tower above Capua he
threatened them all, and would infallibly have defeated
them had they departed from their defensive system.

CHAP. V.

THE time of the elections having arrived, Fabius repaired to Rome to hold the Comitia.

The consuls chosen were Fabius and Marcellus, and great as were the exertions of the past year, those of the present were greater still. Six new legions were raised, so that the Republic maintained in all twenty legions, which, at the opening of the campaign, were thus disposed:—

	Legions.
Sicily, Sardinia, Spain, and Cisalpine Gaul, each employed two legions	8
The consul Fabius took command of a newly raised force at Cales, consisting of	2
Marcellus had the late army of Fabius at Suessula .	2
Gracchus was with his old army of slaves and allies at Luceria, watching Hannibal	2
The prætor Fabius, son of the consul, succeeded M. Valerius in command of the force in Southern Apulia, consisting of .	2
M. Valerius commanded the fleet and the legion which formed the garrison of Tarentum during the preceding year, and was occupied with preparations for his expedition into Greece	1
Varro commanded new levies in Picenum	1
The garrison of Rome	2
Total . . .	20

The Capuans, alarmed by these great preparations, sent to beg Hannibal to come to their defence, who immediately quitted Arpi, and occupied his old quarters on Mount Tifata. Thence, leaving a portion of his force to guard the camp, he swooped down on Puteoli near Neapolis; but finding it too strongly fortified to admit of its capture, he ravaged the territories of Cumæ and Neapolis. While on this expedition, he received a deputation composed of the most influential citizens of Tarentum, offering to deliver the town to him if he would march into their country.

The object of Hannibal during this year was to establish his authority firmly in Campania, and to make that province the base of his operations against Rome. For this purpose, it was necessary to deprive the Romans of a point d'appui such as Nola afforded them, and to reduce the seaport towns of Cumæ and Neapolis, so as to be in constant communication with Carthage.

Hannibal therefore ordered Hanno, who commanded a force of 17,000 infantry, nearly all Bruttian and Lucanian levies, and 1200 Numidian cavalry, in Bruttium, to join him in Campania; and as the direct road was blocked by Nola and by the army of Marcellus, Hanno received instructions to march by Beneventum. Hannibal's design was, so soon as he should receive this accession of strength, to besiege Nola, Neapolis, and Cumæ in succession, employing one army in the siege and another in covering that operation.

To prevent Hanno from reinforcing Hannibal, Fabius ordered Gracchus to move from Luceria to Beneventum; the place of the latter was to be supplied by Fabius the

Younger, who was to advance with his force from the neighbourhood of Tarentum. *

Gracchus reached Beneventum just in time to learn that Hanno had arrived on the very same day, and was encamped on the Calor river, about three miles from the city. Gracchus therefore approached the enemy, and encamped for that night at the distance of a mile from him. His force was composed principally of volunteer slaves, and having promised them their freedom, provided they were victorious in the coming battle, he formed his troops at sunrise next morning, and attacked the enemy, whose defeat was so decisive that only Hanno with 2000 men escaped from the field.

Gracchus, after keeping his promise to his slaves by declaring them free with much solemnity, marched into Lucania to prevent Hanno from assembling another army in that province.

Hannibal's plan of operations in Campania being altogether disconcerted by this catastrophe, he turned his attention to Tarentum, and after having waited in Campania long enough for the Capuans to get in their harvest safely, he set off on his march into Apulia: but he arrived before Tarentum too late; for three days earlier, a Roman officer of rank, sent by the prætor Valerius from Brundusium, had entered the city, encouraged the partisans of Rome, and awed the disaffected, so that when Hannibal made his appearance no movement was made in his favour. With excellent policy, he spared the Tarentine territory, and after sweeping up

* See Observation 2.

all the corn from the neighbourhood of Metapontum and Heraclea, he returned northwards and took up his winter quarters at Salapia.

Meanwhile, Fabius the consul had taken advantage of Hannibal's absence to besiege Casilinum, and as the Capuans from their proximity might annoy the besieging force, Marcellus came from Nola to observe Capua and to cover the siege. The place was garrisoned by 700 of Hannibal's veterans, and by 2000 Capuans; but it surrendered after an obstinate defence, on condition that the garrison should be allowed to retire to Capua. But Marcellus appears to have acted with treachery, and having seized the gate through which the garrison was defiling, killed many, and sent the rest as prisoners to Rome.

After this, Marcellus returned to Nola, while Fabius, the consul, advanced into Samnium, combining his operations with his son in Apulia, and with Gracchus in Lucania. Hanno had withdrawn into Bruttium, and the three Roman armies ravaged the country far and wide wherever it had submitted to Hannibal, and regained the towns of Telesia and Compsa in Samnium, of Blanda in Lucania, and of Œcæ in Apulia, besides taking or killing 25,000 of Hannibal's adherents. They then went into winter quarters: Fabius in his old position at Suessula, Marcellus at Nola, Gracchus in Lucania, and Fabius the prætor at Herdonea in Apulia, watching Hannibal.

In the course of this year, Hieronymus, successor to Hiero king of Syracuse, who had deserted the Roman cause, was slain by his subjects, and the Roman alliance was restored: but a fresh revolution had placed the partisans of Carthage at the head of the government, and Syracuse finally declared war, and attacked the Roman troops. Several other cities followed the example, and the Roman dominion in the island was in danger. Marcellus was therefore sent to Sicily with his two legions to meet the threatening storm.

In another quarter, Philip king of Macedon had prepared everything for a descent on Italy; but previous to embarking he besieged Apollonia, on the west coast of Illyria: M. Valerius, informed of this, sailed from Brundusium, entered Apollonia, dispersed the Macedonian army in a sally, and burnt the fleet which had been prepared for the expedition. Philip returned into Macedon with a dispirited army, and danger from that quarter was for the present averted.

In Spain, also, the two Scipios had gained two great victories during the year, retaken Saguntum, and, after strengthening the defences, had recalled to the town such of the inhabitants as had survived the siege of the year 218 B.C.

SEVENTH CAMPAIGN.

The consuls chosen for this year were Gracchus and Q. Fabius, son of the consul, who had been prætor in the preceding year. The distribution of the Roman forces was as follows:—

Legions.

Gracchus, in Lucania, continued in command of his two
    legions 2

Fabius, who had wintered at Herdonea watching Hannibal,
    kept his old command in Apulia 2

M. Emilius, prætor, commanded two legions likewise in Apulia,
    having his head quarters at Luceria 2

Cn. Fulvius, prætor, succeeded Fabius the elder in command
    of the army at Suessula 2

Varro still remained in Picenum 1

In Sicily two armies were employed, one commanded by Mar-
    cellus, the other by P. Lentulus 4

P. Sempronius in Cisalpine Gaul 2

Q. Mucius in Sardinia 2

P. Scipio in Spain 2

Garrison of Rome 2

Employed in Greece under M. Valerius 1

Total 22

It is impossible clearly to make out the operations of
the present year. Early in the season, Fabius the
consul, with whom his father acted as his lieutenant,
surprised Arpi: the inhabitants who were instrumental
in aiding the Romans to gain the city, returned to their
allegiance, and 1000 Spaniards of the garrison joined
Fabius and fought in the Roman ranks to the end of
the war. Hannibal had wintered at Salapia, and by
turning to the map it will be now seen how hazardous
was his position. With one Roman army at Arpi,
another at Herdonea which might have advanced to
Canusium, these two towns forming safe points of
operation for these armies respectively, and having the
army of Gracchus in Lucania, which might have been
called up to complete the girdle by taking post across

the road to Tarentum behind the Aufidus river, it certainly appears as if the war should have been terminated in that corner of Italy; but we are judging in ignorance of many facts, and Hannibal's superiority in cavalry enabled him to do many things which would otherwise have been impossible.

Unmolested by his numerous enemies, Hannibal marched to Tarentum, and passed the whole summer in the neighbourhood of that town, in the hope of its being delivered up to him by the inhabitants. Capua was thus left to its own resources; but nothing seems to have been undertaken against that city.*

Meanwhile, Gracchus was engaged in Lucania in a partisan warfare, the result of which was the reduction of a few villages and castles.

In Bruttium, a reaction had commenced in favour of Rome; but a Roman contractor or prefect in that province, who had been empowered to raise soldiers, was rash enough to engage with his raw levies in an action against Hanno, and was defeated and made prisoner; which checked the reaction in Bruttium for the time.

In Spain nothing important occurred, except that Syphax, king of Numidia, transferred his alliance from Carthage to Rome, and sent orders to such of his troops as were serving in the Carthaginian armies in Spain, to go over to the Roman generals.

In Sicily a violent struggle was being carried on, and the siege of Syracuse, made famous by the genius and death of Archimedes, was commenced.

* See Observation 3.

In the course of the winter, the town of Tarentum was taken by Hannibal through the connivance of the inhabitants; but the citidel was still held by a Roman garrison.

EIGHTH CAMPAIGN.

The consuls of the year were Fulvius Flaccus and Appius Claudius. So great had been the drain on the population, that it was impossible to recruit the Roman armies with soldiers of the regulated age. Two Commissions were appointed the one to visit all the country tribes within fifty miles of Rome, and the other, such as were more remote, to pass in review every free-born citizen, and to enlist all who were physically not incapable, even below the age of seventeen.

The requirements of the army having been thus satisfied, Q. Fulvius, one consul, succeeded to the command of the army of Fabius in Apulia, while the other, Appius Claudius, took command of that of the ex-prætor Fulvius, at Suessula.

Gracchus was still in Lucania with his two legions holding Hanno in check.

Claudius Nero, now first mentioned, guarded the camp above Suessula with two legions which Varro had raised in Picenum; while the army of Appius Claudius, the consul, marched to Bovianum, and there united with that of the other consul from Apulia.

Cn. Fulvius Flaccus, brother of the consul, as prætor, succeeded the ex-prætor M. Emilius in the command of his two legions in Apulia.

The same forces were employed under the same commanders in Sicily, Sardinia, Cisalpine Gaul, Spain, and Greece, as during the preceding year; and in addition, a force of two legions under the prætor, M. Junius, was sent into Etruria, as that province was suspected of disaffection. Including the usual garrison of Rome, two legions, the Republic maintained during this present year twenty-five legions.

After the capture of Tarentum, Hannibal armed the citizens and made an attempt to take the citadel, but its position rendering it impregnable by assault, because it was surrounded on three sides by the sea, and on the fourth side, separated from the town by a wide and deep cut through which the sea flowed, he raised a line of contravallation on the land side; but he could not blockade the garrison without the presence of a strong Carthaginian fleet to close the mouth of the harbour, the entrance to which was very narrow and completely commanded by the citadel.

The armies of the two consuls were, as has been said, united at Bovianum, apparently with the intention of reducing Samnium, but really to mature their preparations for the siege of Capua. Hannibal's absence in Apulia had left the Campanian territory at the mercy of the Roman armies; the Capuans had been unable to sow their lands, they were already suffering from want, and suspecting the intention of the consuls, they now sent to Hannibal to inform him that they could not hope to make a long defence unless he should take steps to provision their city.

Hannibal thereupon ordered Hanno to march with

his army from Bruttium to the neighbourhood of Beneventum, to perform that service. It was a hazardous
operation, for Gracchus was in Lucania*, and Nero at
Suessula, on the flank of Hanno's line of march; yet it
was accomplished without accident, and Hanno arrived
at Beneventum before his enemies appear to have been
aware of his having moved at all; and having encamped
within three miles of the town, he sent word to the
Capuans to send to him every carriage and beast of
burden they could lay their hands on, to carry home the
corn he was about to collect. He then caused the corn
which was stored in all the friendly towns of that district
to be forwarded to his camp, and swept up all the grain
from the surrounding country. Hanno fulfilled his
part of the contract, but the Capuans failed in theirs;
they did not send nearly sufficient transport, and Hanno
was consequently detained in a position which every
hour was becoming more perilous. For Beneventum
being a Latin colony, the garrison had sent word to the
consuls at Bovianum (only thirty miles distant) of the
arrival of Hanno. Fulvius with his army set out
instantly, entered Beneventum by night, learnt on his
arrival that the Capuans had at last sent the required
transport, that the Carthaginian camp was crowded and
confused with cattle, carriages, and non-combatants,
and that Hanno with part of his force was absent,
scouring the country for more plunder.

Fulvius marched out of the city next morning at daybreak, stormed the camp of the Carthaginians, slaughtered great numbers of them, and captured all the

* See Observation 4.

supplies which had been amassed with so much pains; and Hanno on hearing that the object of his expedition was totally frustrated, retired with the remnant of his force into Bruttium.*

After this catastrophe, the Capuans sent again a pressing entreaty for succour to Hannibal. Their negligence had just cost him an army and had frustrated all his pains for their relief; but with unmoved good temper he promised not to forget them, and sent back 2000 of his invincible cavalry to protect their lands from the ravages of the enemy. It was of importance to him not to quit the south till a later period, for since he had taken Tarentum, the neighbouring cities of Metapontum, Heraclea, and Thurii, had joined him; he had before won Croton and Locri, so that he was now master of every place on the coast from the Straits of Messana to the mouth of the Adriatic, except Rhegium and the citadel of Tarentum.

The Roman fleet had just thrown a plentiful supply of provisions into the latter, and he desired to gain these two places before he moved northward, so as to leave behind him a wide and secure base of operations, from all points of which he could communicate with Carthage and Macedon by sea.

The battle of Beneventum, in destroying the army of Hanno, rendered that of Gracchus disposable to co-operate in the intended siege of Capua. That general therefore received orders to leave his heavy infantry in some well fortified position to overawe Lucania, and to repair to Beneventum with his cavalry and light

* See Observation 5.

infantry. This measure would raise the aggregate
force of the Roman cavalry, the arm in which the deficiency was always the most felt, to 7000 horses.
While Gracchus was preparing to comply he was killed
in an ambuscade ; and the cavalry alone, under Cornelius his quæstor, marched towards Beneventum; for
the infantry, being principally composed of the slaves
whom Gracchus had enfranchised, thought themselves
absolved by the death of their deliverer from further
service, and immediately dispersed to their homes.

Thus Lucania was left without any Roman force, until
M. Centenius, an old centurion who possessed great
strength, courage, and force of character, without military skill, offered to command there if the senate would
intrust him with a force equal to a single legion. He
obtained his wish, and being a popular soldier, his numbers were swelled on his march by volunteers to near
16,000 men, with whom he arrived in Lucania; where
we leave him for the present, in the expectation that
Hannibal will give a good account of him bye and bye.

Meanwhile the consuls, being ignorant of the presence
of Hannibal's cavalry, approached Capua for the purpose of commencing the siege ; they entered the great
Campanian plain by the Caudine Forks, and separated
into small dispersed parties to gather such corn as had
been sown which was still green. Hannibal's cavalry
sallied out upon them and inflicted a severe loss, but
the Romans were too strong to be impeded in their
design — their two armies encamped before Capua, and
had the harvest of the whole country in their power.
It is stated that a few days later, Hannibal astonished

the Roman generals by appearing once more in his old position on the summit of Mount Tifata; that he descended thence and entered the city; that two days after he marched out and offered battle, which the Romans accepted; and that the contest was doubtful until the appearance of a fresh body of cavalry on the flank of both armies, namely, that which Cornelius was bringing from the late army of Gracchus, decided both parties to sound the retreat, each being ignorant whether the new comers were friends or foes.*

After this combat, the consuls desiring to draw Hannibal to a distance from Capua, separated their forces, and marched, Fulvius to the neighbourhood of Cumæ, Appius towards Apulia. Hannibal decided on following the latter. It may well be conceived how great was the rejoicing in Capua when the morning sun revealed the absence of their dreaded enemies, and with what gratitude and admiration the citizens gazed on their deliverer. "But almost within sight and hearing of their joy, the stern old Fulvius was crouching as it were in his thicket, watching the moment for a second spring upon his prey; and when Hannibal left that rejoicing and admiring multitude to follow the traces of Appius, he passed through the gates of Capua to enter them again no more."†

Hannibal pursued Appius, but no details exist of the march of the latter. He eluded Hannibal, probably by turning short round to his left, and marching round by Allifæ and the Valley of the Vulturnus, returned to

* See Observation 6.   † Arnold.

Capua by Casilinum. Hannibal proceeded towards Tarentum, but found his passage barred by Centenius and the force he had collected to replace that of Gracchus. Centenius was killed, and his army destroyed in the engagement he so rashly sought; and Hannibal then marched against the prætor Fulvius, who lay near Herdonea, being induced to do so by a knowledge of the vain and indolent character of that general, and of the loose discipline he maintained among his troops. Fulvius had about 18,000 men, and though far inferior in numbers to the enemy, his soldiers were eager to fight. Hannibal, informed of the spirit they were in, knew that he might choose his own field of battle, secure of being attacked. He accordingly posted 3000 light infantry in ambush behind the brushwood and hedges in the neighbourhood of the field of battle, and ordered Mago to place himself with 2000 Numidian cavalry during the action on the enemy's line of retreat. At day-break he then formed his army in front of his camp. Fulvius marched out immediately and formed opposite in one thin line, in order not to be outflanked by Hannibal, who was still very superior in numbers, notwithstanding the detachments he had made. The Romans hardly sustained the first shock; surrounded by Hannibal's ambuscade, and their retreat cut off by Mago's horse, their army was destroyed, and hardly 2000 men escaped from the field.

Thus within a few weeks three armies were lost to Rome, viz. that of Gracchus and the two which Hannibal had defeated; and her hold on Southern Italy was gone.

Notwithstanding these successes, we are told that Hannibal returned to Tarentum *, and being disappointed in his expectation of the surrender of the citadel, as well as in a belief that Brundisium would be betrayed into his hands, he remained inactive in Apulia during the remainder of the year, while the consuls resumed their operations against Capua. Three great magazines had been formed for the supply of the besieging force at Casilinum, Puteoli, and the fort of Vulturnum, at the mouth of the Vulturnus river, all of which were conveniently replenished by sea with corn brought from Ostia, whither it had previously been collected from Sardinia and Etruria. The disbanded infantry of Gracchus too was re-assembled and added to the armies of the consuls; Claudius Nero was summoned from his camp at Suessula, and the three armies began the great work of surrounding Capua with double continuous lines of contra and circumvallation, to repel the sorties of the garrison, and the attempts Hannibal might make to relieve it. The works were not completed till late in the winter; all the attempts of the Capuans to delay them were unavailing; and early in the year 211 B.C. they sent out a Numidian, who succeeded in passing the lines and reaching Hannibal with a pressing entreaty for help.

Towards the end of the year 212 B.C., Syracuse was taken by Marcellus, and a Roman fleet surprised in the port of Utica 130 corn ships, the capture of which afforded a seasonable supply to the Roman forces in Sicily, which were beginning to suffer from want.

* See Observation 7.

The war in Spain was marked during the same year by the defeat and death of the two Scipios, and by the withdrawal of the Roman forces behind the Ebro, whither they were pursued by the victorious Carthaginians commanded by Hasdrubal; who were, however, compelled to recross the Ebro by the valour and ability of a young Roman knight, L. Marcius, who had been raised to the command of the Roman army on the death of their leaders by the unanimous voice of the soldiers.

OBSERVATIONS ON THE THREE PRECEDING CAMPAIGNS.

1. In all of these campaigns the policy of the Roman
commanders was to keep Hannibal constantly watched
by two, sometimes three, armies, while others were
employed in opposing his lieutenants in Lucania and
Bruttium. Thus, on the opening of the campaign of
214, Hannibal, in his camp on Mount Tifata, had Marcellus on the one hand at Suessula, Fabius on the other
at Cales, while Gracchus opposed Hanno in Lucania,
and the prætor, Fabius the younger, was with another
army in Apulia. It will be observed that the policy
which was steadily pursued by the Roman generals to
the end of the war, with the exception of two rash and
incapable men, was to wear out Hannibal's troops with
fatiguing marches and continued petty skirmishes, and
never to engage in any combat unless the chances of
success were greatly in their favour.

By such a warfare, Hannibal, abandoned by the
suicidal folly of Carthage to his own resources, saw his
troops melting from him by degrees. His own force
was constantly diminishing, while that opposed to him
never numbered less than 80,000 men. That he should
have been able to maintain the struggle so long is due
solely to his personal genius; and it is indeed wonderful
to see him not merely maintaining the struggle, but
marching and encamping where he pleased without let

or hindrance, his presence being the signal either for the total destruction of the opposing armies or for their hurried retreat.

2. The march of Gracchus to Beneventum was a fine strategical movement, ordered by Fabius to prevent Hannibal from being reinforced by Hanno. Thus both the roads from Lucania to Capua were blocked up, that by the sea coast being barred by the garrison of Nola. The movement of Gracchus and consequent defeat of Hanno obliged Hannibal to change all his plans.

It is true that even when reinforced by Hanno Hannibal's force would have been far inferior to the aggregate number of the Romans, but he would have been able to employ one army in siege operations, and to cover it with the other, quite secure that his great and unfailing superiority in cavalry would in that plain country enable him to defy all the attempts of the united forces of the enemy.

It will be observed that from this time the Romans maintained a force in Lucania to hold Hanno in check.

3. It cannot be believed that the numerous Roman armies should have been so unprofitably directed by the sagacity of Fabius as appears from the only existing accounts of this campaign. Hannibal, according to those accounts, lingered in the neighbourhood of Tarentum; yet the armies of Fabius and Emilius, in Apulia, neither attempted to impede his operations against Tarentum nor to besiege Capua which was left to its own resources. Gracchus, with a third army, was unprofitably employed in Lucania, while Cn. Fulvius lay

inactive in his camp above Suessula. Under such circumstances the Roman course was clear, viz. to push the siege of Capua with all their strength, and to prevent Hannibal from marching to its relief. The latter object should have been effected by entrenching several very strong positions on the road by which Hannibal must approach Capua, particularly the defile of the Caudine Forks through which an army coming from Beneventum must pass to enter the Campanian plain, and by appointing one army to oppose Hannibal's approach in these positions, while the other three armies carried on the siege. Hannibal's old camp on the summit of Mount Tifata should have been made very strong, and defended by a detachment of the besieging force, which should have been reinforced whenever it was known that Hannibal was approaching. The covering army would likewise, if either forced or turned by Hannibal, retire on that camp. With these dispositions, had Hannibal descended into the plain and attacked the besiegers, the army on Tifata would have descended on his flank or rear. It is inconceivable that the Roman generals should have taken no steps to prevent Hannibal from returning to his old camp on Tifata whenever it suited his purpose. But the history of these campaigns is very obscure, and although it is good practice for the military student to study the operations as related, and to remark on their faults, he cannot feel sure that the operations are correctly reported, and consequently that the faults were really committed at all.

4. Gracchus must have been very deficient in vigilance

and his light cavalry very useless, to permit a hostile army of 18,000 men to pass him and to gain his communications.   His intelligence too must have been very defective that he did not even learn Hanno's departure from Lucania in time to follow him up and interrupt his foraging.

Napoleon says, if a general in command of an army is not well supplied with intelligence, it is because he is ignorant of his trade.

5. Hanno knew that Beneventum was hostile and that the garrison would immediately send word of his appearance to the consuls.   He should therefore have pushed parties of light horse to a sufficient distance on the roads by which an enemy might approach, to enable him to be prepared for attack.   Under no circumstances should he have been absent from his camp, or such a surprise have been possible as that which resulted in the destruction of his army and the capture of the supplies whereon depended the fate of Capua.

6. No reliance can be placed on this account.   If the Roman generals allowed Hannibal to occupy his camp at Tifata and to enter Capua unmolested, it is little to their credit.   They accepted battle two days later; why then did they not attack Hannibal in his march to enter the town?

7. It appears strange that Hannibal should have retired into a remote corner of Apulia just at the moment when the dispersion of the army of Gracchus, speedily followed by the destruction of two other Roman armies, must be supposed to have raised the spirit of his

own troops and proportionally depressed the Romans,—
at the moment of Capua's greatest need which it must
naturally be supposed he would have chosen to strike
his hardest blows. Although we have no distinct statement of his motives we may imagine that some were
furnished by the internal state of his army, and others
are not difficult to discover.

There were still three Roman armies around Capua.
Hannibal did not possess a single sea port town in Campania. His army, though always victorious must have
been gradually diminishing, and sorely in need of reinforcements; desertions had taken place; he would have
found it difficult to provision his army during the winter
on Mount Tifata, as the country must have been ruined
from having been so long the seat of war; and to have
drawn its subsistence from Capua would have done that
city more harm than his presence would have com-
pensated.

A march to Capua at this time, since he could not
remain there, would have been useless. The Romans
would not have given him an opportunity to strike a
damaging blow, and he must eventually have gone
southwards, after having uselessly fatigued his troops.

He probably acted on a profound calculation of the
chances, and knowing that Capua could sustain a long
siege, placed his hopes for its relief principally on the
arrival of reinforcements from Carthage which would
have enabled him to take the offensive with effect; he
therefore retired to the south, where he possessed the
whole coast and would be in a position to receive the ex-

pected reinforcements as well as to feed his present troops. And it is worthy of remark here that if Hasdrubal could have gone by sea to the south of Italy, in place of being obliged to march through Cisalpine Gaul, the accession of strength which his arrival would have brought to Hannibal would not only have enabled him to relieve Capua, but perhaps to reduce Rome to the very brink of ruin.

CHAP. VI.

NINTH CAMPAIGN.

THE consuls for the year were Cn. Fulvius, who had
been prætor two years before (not that Cn. Fulvius who
was defeated at Herdonea), and P. Sulpicius. They
remained at Rome for some time to organise their
troops, and eventually passed into Apulia with the two
legions of liberated slaves which had dispersed at the
death of Gracchus but had been re-assembled, and the
two legions which had formed the city garrison during
the preceding year. The late consuls Appius and
Fulvius continued to direct the siege of Capua as pro-
consuls, and were ordered not to quit the place until it
surrendered. Claudius Nero with his two legions continued at Capua under the orders of the consuls.
Thus six legions were employed before that place.

The same forces continued to be employed in Etruria,
in Cisalpine Gaul, Spain, Sicily, and Sardinia—the total
number of legions maintained being twenty-five—the
same as the preceding year.

At the commencement of this campaign no army
was immediately opposed to Hannibal in Apulia, as it
was thought urgent not to recall the troops from
Etruria or Cisalpine Gaul. And in Sicily the siege of

Syracuse being just terminated, it was of great importance to Rome to complete the conquest of that island.

The citadel of Tarentum was well provisioned and
safe for the present. The lines before Capua were
finished, and were sufficiently strong to enable the
besieging force of 70,000 men to withstand the efforts
of Hannibal from without, and those of the garrison
from within.

Meanwhile the Capuans awaited with anxious hope
the appearance of their great ally. They made constant
sorties, but although their cavalry always had the
advantage against the Roman cavalry, their infantry
was decidedly inferior and they could not therefore
hope to force the Roman lines. The constant inferiority of the Roman cavalry led to the more
perfect organisation of the Roman light infantry, which
was composed of the strongest and most supple and
active youths to be found in the army. This force
which now first received the name of " velites," was
armed the same as before, viz. with a small round
shield and with seven darts of four feet in length
having sharp iron points. The velites by constant
training came at length to be able to act with the
cavalry; accompanying them " en croupe" in their
changes of position, and even during the charge, on the
first shock of which they jumped to the ground and
gliding between and under the horses annoyed the
enemy with their darts. It is said that in the cavalry
fight which the Romans provoked after this new organisation of the light troops, the Capuans, disconcerted
by the novelty of such a mode of fighting, were com-

pletely defeated, and that they never afterwards regained their ascendancy.

The garrison was already reduced to great straits when the Numidian despatched from Capua reached Hannibal near Tarentum, as has been already related. Hannibal, leaving his heavy baggage and weakly men behind, now set out by forced marches for Capua; but the essence of his movement being to surprise the besiegers, he was obliged to make a long round to avoid Beneventum; proceeding therefore down the valley of the Calor to the Vulturnus he arrived in a valley behind Mount Tifata. He forthwith sent off several messengers to endeavour separately to penetrate through the Roman lines into the city during the night, and to appoint an hour on the following day for a combined attack by himself and the garrison on the besiegers. One of these messengers succeeded in entering the city, and at the hour appointed on the next day, to the great astonishment of the consuls, Hannibal suddenly appeared marching to assault their entrenchments, while the garrison at the same time made a desperate attack from the town. The besiegers however were sufficiently numerous to oppose both attacks, which were indeed almost hopeless on strong entrenchments defended by Roman infantry; and Hannibal, perceiving that he was powerless to assist the Capuans by direct means, and that his stay in their neighbourhood was useless, took a resolution which might either oblige the Romans to raise the siege, or accomplish a still greater object: he resolved to march on Rome.

Having lighted his camp fires on Mount Tifata, and

despatched a Numidian, who on pretence of being a deserter, should gain access to the Roman lines and thence into the city, to encourage the besieged to hold out at least until the issue of his great stroke became known,—Hannibal left his camp at nightfall, and the next morning when the Romans were preparing to encounter a second assault, he and his army were far away.

The direction of his march is supposed to have been through Samnium by Æsernia, through the Pelignian territory, and by the north shore of Lake Fucinus; thus, passing under the walls of Alba, Hannibal approached Rome, crossed the Anio River and encamped at the distance of eight miles from the city.

When Fulvius discovered the sudden departure of Hannibal, he penetrated his design and sent an express to Rome to warn the senate. Opinions in that body were divided. Some proposed to order up for the defence of the city not only the forces which were besieging Capua, but all the other armies in Italy; but Fabius strongly opposed so pusillanimous a measure, and represented to the senate that it would be shameful to allow themselves to be terrified into the very course which Hannibal most wished them to follow, viz. the raising of the siege of Capua. The utmost he would consent to was that Fulvius at the head of a picked force of 15,000 infantry and 1000 cavalry, should repair to Rome to oppose Hannibal, leaving 50,000 men to maintain the blockade.

Owing to the interior lines on which the Romans moved, it so happened that Fulvius entered Rome by

one road on the very day on which Hannibal arrived
within eight miles of the city by another. The regular
garrison consisted of two legions which had been just
enrolled under the consuls; besides these there were
the legions which had dispersed at the death of Gracchus; and the town of Alba on witnessing the march of
Hannibal, had sent off its whole force to aid in the defence of the city. Thus the town was too strongly
defended to be attacked with the slightest prospect of
success.

The day after, Hannibal advanced his camp to within
five miles of Rome on the left bank of the Anio, and
pushed a reconnaissance to the very gates of the city,
but retired to his camp after a skirmish with the Roman
troops. Fabius and Fulvius encamped with their forces
outside the walls, but Hannibal could not provoke them
to risk a general action. He indemnified himself for
his disappointment by plundering and devastating the
country around his camp, and expected anxiously to
hear that his diversion in favour of Capua had been
successful. But learning now that the blockade was
nothing relaxed, he saw that he had missed his stroke,
and prepared to retire. He could no longer avert the
fall of Capua, and though it must have cost him a
severe struggle to leave that place to its fate, the importance of the interests which were at stake in the
south decided him to proceed to Apulia.* The consuls
followed him in his march to harass his rear, while
Fulvius returned with his command to Capua. The
consuls attacked Hannibal during his passage of the

* See Observation 1.

Anio of which the bridges had been broken down, captured a great part of the booty he had accumulated and inflicted severe loss in men. To rid himself of his pursuers, Hannibal turned fiercely upon them after a few days' march, and assaulted their camp in the night. The Romans were driven from it with loss and rallied in a strong position in the mountains. Hannibal pursued the rest of his march unmolested, and passing rapidly through Lucania made a sudden swoop on Rhegium in the hope of surprising that place; but failing in this, he returned to give some rest to his army in the neighbourhood of Tarentum, the citadel of which place still held out.

Here he heard of the surrender of Capua, the garrison of which was absolutely starving, and hopeless of relief.

Yet, notwithstanding this great success, the Romans had no great cause for exultation. Never had the invincibility of Hannibal been more fully proved than in this campaign. He had overrun half Italy, crossed and recrossed the Apennines, advanced to the very gates of Rome, and wasted her territory; that sacred territory which had not been profaned by the foot of an enemy, save as a prisoner, for 150 years. He had passed backwards and forwards through the midst of hostile armies, yet no superiority of numbers, no advantage of ground had ever emboldened the Romans to meet him in the field. He possessed now a perfectly secure base of operations in the south.

Etruria was discontented, and required the presence of two legions; even the Latin colonies, impatient of the continued heavy burthen of the war, showed signs of discontent; in Spain, the recent defeat and death of the two Scipios left Hasdrubal free to carry his genius and his arms to the aid of his brother. And if Hasdrubal had now landed his army in the southern part of Italy, it might have changed the fate of the world.

The fall of Capua was the last important event of the campaign of 211. Claudius Nero with his two legions was sent to Spain to succeed the Scipios.

TENTH CAMPAIGN.

In the spring of 210, Marcellus, who was recalled from Sicily towards the close of the last year, and M. Valerius, were elected consuls. The latter was absent in Greece, employed against Philip of Macedon, against whom before he returned home he concluded an alliance offensive and defensive with the Ætolians, and thus left him quite enough to do to defend his own dominions, without thinking of an invasion of Italy. The war taxes pressed with great severity on the citizens and colonies of Rome, but this year increased demands were made on them, and there was much and general discontent. The senate being assembled, was told by Valerius, now returned, that before the people should be called on to make great sacrifices, the higher classes should set the example; he proposed that every senator should devote to the public service the whole of the gold and silver in his possession excepting a very small quantity to serve for ornaments to his wife and daughters, and for the use of his table. The senate so thoroughly shared the spirit of the speaker that it thanked him for his suggestion, and at the conclusion of the sitting the members of that body crowded to the forum, followed by slaves bearing their gold and silver, and contended for the honour of being the first to deposit their offerings. The example was irresistible ; it descended through the different ranks, all classes poured in their contributions, and the treasury was far more effectually and more politicly replenished by the free-will offering of the whole people than could have been done by any tax.

The forces in Italy were thus distributed : Marcellus commanded two legions in Samnium; Cn. Fulvius as proconsul, a like force in Apulia. The proconsul Q. Fulvius, remained with two legions at Capua. Etruria, Cisalpine Gaul, Spain and Sicily employed the same number of troops as heretofore, and Marcus Valerius, the consul, commanded in Sicily. In Apulia, the town of Salapia was delivered up to the Romans, and 500 Numidians who composed the garrison were all killed or made prisoners. In Samnium, Marcellus made himself master of two small towns, and captured 3000 of Hannibal's soldiers, besides large stores of corn and barley. Meanwhile Cn. Fulvius encamped before Herdonea, in the hope of gaining that town, which revolted from Rome after Cannæ. Hannibal, as usual, received perfect information of the enemy's proceedings through his spies, and having learnt that Cn. Fulvius was in correspondence with some of the citizens of Herdonea, and that he kept very lax discipline in his camp, he advanced from

Bruttium, whither he had retired after the fall of Salapia, by forced marches to Herdonea, attacked and dispersed the army of Cn. Fulvius, and killed that commander. After this feat, he crossed the mountains into Lucania to look after Marcellus, who had advanced into that province from Samnium. But Marcellus was too cautious to risk a battle; he watched his enemy closely during the remainder of the season which was not marked by any event of importance, and Hannibal returned to winter in the neighbourhood of Tarentum while Marcellus went into quarters in Venusia.

In Sicily the consul M. Valerius had succeeded in completely subduing the island, for which important achievement he was mainly indebted to the assistance of Mutines, an able Numidian officer of Hannibal's, who was induced by the affronts he received from Hanno, occasioned by jealousy, to deliver up Agrigentum to the Romans and to join their cause. Thus the greater part of the force which had been employed in Sicily would become available against Hannibal.

ELEVENTH CAMPAIGN.

The consuls elected for the year were Q. Fulvius and Fabius the elder, the former for the fourth time, the latter for the fifth. The plan of campaign was as follows:

Fabius in command of two legions, was to beseige the town of Tarentum, as the loss of this place would deprive Hannibal of the resources of the surrounding country, and of the most direct point of communication with Philip of Macedon, should fortune favour the operations of that monarch in Greece. It is true that the citadel still holding out against him, Hannibal did not derive the full advantage from the possession of the town that he otherwise would have done, but it was feared the citadel might fall.

Fulvius, the other consul, with two legions which the reduction of Sicily enabled the Romans to withdraw from thence, was to endeavour to recover the towns on the southern coast which were in Hannibal's possession.

Marcellus continued in command of the two legions of which he had made such a prudent use in the preceding year; his business was so to occupy Hannibal as to prevent him from interfering with Fabius at Tarentum. The prætor Crispinus was with two legions in Campania. In Sicily Marcus Valerius commanded as proconsul. He still retained two Roman legions, and organised the Numidians who came over with Mutines and some of the Syracusans for the defence of the island, and sent a party of volunteer adventurers over to Rhegium, who were determined to make an attack on Caulon. Levinus was able moreover to employ constantly thirty vessels in carrying supplies backwards and forwards between Sicily and the army of Fabius before Tarentum.

The remainder of the fleet was employed in guarding the Sicilian coast, in making occasional descents on Africa, and in procuring information of the condition and plans of the enemy.

Intelligence now reached Rome that Hasdrubal was increasing his forces largely in Spain, with the design of leading a large army to the assistance of his brother in

Italy. The dismay occasioned by this news was heightened by the refusal of twelve of the Roman colonies to furnish their contingents towards the expenses and levies of the year, on the plea that they had neither men nor money remaining.

Had this example been followed by the other colonies Rome was lost : it was indeed a terrible crisis. The consuls had not yet left Rome ; everything was left to their discretion, and they exerted their influence so successfully in private with the deputies of the eighteen remaining colonies, that when asked officially if their contingents of men and money were forthcoming, they replied that the contingents were forthcoming, and more if necessary ; adding that whatever order they might receive from the Roman people, they had means enough, and will more than enough to obey.

The consuls took the field, and it was now more than ever necessary to act vigorously against Hannibal, and if possible to cripple him in the south before he could be joined by his brother. Marcellus broke up from Venusia, and proceeded to watch and harass Hannibal. Fabius went to besiege Tarentum. Fulvius marched into Lucania, and Caulon was besieged by the Sicilian volunteers. All the towns which remained to Hannibal in Samnium, and many in Lucania, submitted to the Romans; and while Hannibal allowed himself to be amused by Marcellus in Northern Apulia, the southern coast of Italy which formed his base of operations was in danger of being torn from his grasp.

His genius and energy now shone out with their wonted brilliancy. He turned fiercely on his opponent and so disabled him in two actions, that Marcellus took refuge in Venusia during the remainder of the campaign.

Confiding in the strength and fidelity of Tarentum, he flew now to Caulon, where he captured the whole besieging force.

He then went by forced marches to Tarentum, intending to crush Fabius as he had crushed Marcellus. But when within five miles of the place, he learned that it had been betrayed to Fabius, and that his most important city and best harbour was in the hands of the Romans.

Notwithstanding this reverse, Hannibal, during the remainder of the campaign, appears to have been completely master of the open country, marching, burning, and destroying where he pleased, without let or hindrance.

The Romans were much disappointed at the general result of the season's operations; for although they had recovered Tarentum, another army had been destroyed by Hannibal; and Marcellus shared the fate of all unsuccessful commanders in being plentifully abused, and doubtless called an old woman by the " Times " of the day; it was even proposed to deprive him of his command. Marcellus in defence said he had done his best — that he had twice fought with Hannibal to prevent him from marching into Bruttium, and that he ought not justly to be blamed if, in common with all other Roman commanders, he had failed to overcome Hannibal. His defence appeared so reasonable, that he was not only continued in his command, but was elected consul for the ensuing year, and with him, Crispinus, the ex-prætor.

TWELFTH CAMPAIGN.

In Spain, during the year just terminated, the inhabitants had nearly all abandoned the Carthaginian alliance; Hasdrubal had been defeated by Scipio the younger, afterwards called Africanus, who succeeded his father in the command of the Roman forces in Spain, and who now acquired the complete mastery of the whole southern coast of the peninsula. Hasdrubal, after his defeat, retired across the Tagus with the intention of passing into Gaul over the western extremity of the Pyrenees, and thence into Italy.*

Meanwhile the increased contributions which the exigencies of the war had compelled the Romans to demand of their allies, joined probably to the rumours of Hasdrubal's intended march and the intrigues of Hannibal, had increased the disaffection among the Etruscans. In addition to the two legions which had been maintained in that province, a third was sent to Arretium, which was the focus of the sedition, under Varro.

The situation of the Roman armies at the commencement of the campaign was as follows :—

The two consuls, Marcellus in command of his own army, and Crispinus with that of Fulvius, were opposed to Hannibal in Apulia.

* See Observation 6.

Q. Claudius, with the two legions which Fabius had commanded in the preceding campaign, occupied Tarentum and the adjacent country.

Fulvius with one legion was at Capua.

The consuls were encamped about three miles east of Venusia; Hannibal about three miles to the south of the Romans. His position seemed now to be full of peril. In his front was an army of 40,000 Romans; on his right rear, another of 20,000 based upon Tarentum. If obliged to retreat, he must do so either on the seaport towns of Metapontum and Heraclea, or into Bruttium, for in all Italy he did not possess a single town besides the two just mentioned, excepting in Bruttium. He could not safely retreat on Metapontum or Heraclea, because the consuls would have harassed his rear, while the Tarentine legions would have taken him in flank. Bruttium therefore was his natural base, and the width of the neck of that peninsula was so narrow that the entrance into it might be easily defended by such a commander as Hannibal against all comers. All the towns of Bruttium too were in his possession, except Rhegium.

Hannibal, in his camp near Venusia, now learnt that an expedition from Sicily was about to besiege Locri, and that one of the legions was destined to march from Tarentum to assist in that expedition. He accordingly sent off 2000 cavalry and 3000 infantry, picked troops, to intercept their march. These, having occupied a favourable position, fell upon the flank of the Romans unawares, killed many, took a large number of prisoners, and drove the remainder back to Tarentum. After this success the detachment returned to Hannibal, who was watching for an opening to strike some decisive blow. Between the hostile camps was a wooded hill which neither of the armies occupied; but Hannibal perceiving that it presented great advantages for an ambuscade, posted a strong party of Numidians in the wood on the slope of the hill towards his side. They were thus completely concealed from the enemy.

It being proposed in the Roman camp to occupy this hill and establish an entrenched post there, both the consuls proceeded to reconnoitre it, attended by a slender escort of cavalry. The Numidians broke out upon them, killed Marcellus, and desperately wounded Crispinus and the younger Marcellus. The legions in the camp saw the surprise but were unable to come to the rescue in time. Crispinus and the young Marcellus rode in, covered with blood, followed by the scattered survivors of the escort; but Marcellus, six times consul, the bravest and stoutest of soldiers, who had dedicated the spoils of the Gaulish king slain by his hand, to Jupiter Feretrius in the Capitol, was lying dead on a nameless hill, and his arms and body were Hannibal's.

Hannibal, on hearing from the Numidians what they had done, instantly put his army in motion and occupied the hill. There he found the body of Marcellus; he looked upon it in silence with deep interest; the soul of the great Carthaginian was moved at the sight of the clay which only a short hour before bore the name of the boldest and most constant of his enemies; and having drawn off the ring from the finger of the body, he ordered, as in the case of Flaminius and Gracchus, that it should be honourably burned, and that the ashes should be sent to Marcellus' son.

The Romans deeply discouraged, retired from the neighbourhood of their terrible enemy. The army of Marcellus to the shelter of Venusia, that of Crispinus to Capua, where that consul died of his wounds. Hannibal then turned to relieve Locri, an object which was effected by the mere terror of his approach. The besieging force hastily re-embarked, leaving their siege artillery and stores to the enemy.

During the remainder of the year, Hannibal's supremacy was undisputed by any army in the field; and now in the course of the autumn, messengers from Marseilles brought word to Rome that Hasdrubal, who, after crossing the Tagus, had turned the sources of the Ebro, and entered Gaul by the same line as was followed by the Duke of Wellington after the battle of Vittoria, was busily engaged in recruiting in Gaul. A little later, information was received that he had completed his levies and that he waited only for the melting of the snows to cross the Alps; his arrival in Italy might therefore be expected in the following spring.

Rome must therefore prepare to meet a second son of Hamilcar in Italy; and if she had found it so difficult to maintain the contest against one, how could she hope successfully to oppose two? and at the very time when her most tried commanders were either dead or enfeebled by age.

THIRTEENTH CAMPAIGN.

The public voice pronounced that the fittest man to choose as consul was Claudius Nero, who had already held important commands during several successive years. And as his colleague, was chosen after some hesitation, Marcus Livius, a stern and sullen old man, who had done good service as consul against the Illyrians twelve years before, but who at that time had been unjustly accused of peculation and fined for the offence. The sense of the shame and the wrong were intolerable to him, so that he had lived from that time in sullen enmity with all men of his own class, and he nourished an especial feud against Nero.

Livius at first flatly refused the consulship, saying that if he had been justly condemned, he was not a fitting man for that office. But his opposition was at length overcome by the senators, who then besought him to be reconciled to his colleague. This he also resisted, but finally the authority of the senate prevailed, and they were publicly reconciled.

There are pages of English history yet to be written, which will show that the government charged with the selection of the men destined to uphold the honour of England in the command of her armies, did not imitate the wise conduct of the Roman senate on this occasion; and thought it a little matter that officers appointed to high commands, who must be in constant official communication with each other, should yet be on terms of the most rancorous private hostility.

Livius was destined to arrest the progress of Hasdrubal in the north. Besides his own two legions, a second army of two legions commanded by L. Porcius, already in Cisalpine Gaul, was to be under his orders, while a third army of equal strength was in Etruria under Varro.

In the south Hannibal was opposed by three armies, viz. by that which Marcellus had commanded, under Nero in Apulia; by that of Crispinus, under Q. Fulvius; and by the two Tarentine legions, under the ex-prætor Q. Claudius. One legion remained at Capua, and two others formed the garrison of Rome, so that fifteen legions were employed this year in Italy alone.

By this time Hasdrubal had entered Italy; he made an unsuccessful attempt to reduce Placentia, and having waited before that place long enough to be joined by the Gaulish and Ligurian levies, he advanced towards Ariminum, the prætor Porcius retiring before him.

Livius hastened up with his army and joined Porcius at Ariminum, but they afterwards abandoned that place and fell back before Hasdrubal behind the Metaurus, and subsequently behind the Sena River.

Meanwhile, Nero having incorporated the army of Fulvius with his own, commanded an army of 40,000 men; his head quarters were at Venusia, and his task was by any and every means to prevent Hannibal from moving northwards to join his brother.

The movements of Hannibal and the early events of the campaign are involved in doubt; but it is stated that he moved forward from his winter quarters near Locri, first into Lucania, then into Apulia, that he then fell back into Bruttium, and finally advanced once more into Apulia to the neighbourhood of Canusium; that in all these movements he was closely followed and harassed by Nero, and that he lost 15,000 men in several engagements with that general; which last statement may be dismissed as unworthy of belief.

The explanation of these movements probably is, that Hannibal, having 40,000 men in his front, and 20,000 at Tarentum in his rear, besides 10,000 at Capua on his left flank, was not strong enough to move forward into the heart of Italy for the purpose of meeting his brother, without first assembling his garrisons and raising additional soldiers in Bruttium; and he flew from one province to another to effect that object as speedily as possible, as he knew from rumour that Hasdrubal was already on the Po, although he had received no direct tidings from him. It was absolutely necessary that he should receive those tidings before he marched northwards, as Hasdrubal might choose to march from Placentia, either through Etruria or Umbria, and Hannibal's movements must conform to those of his brother.

It was therefore in the hope of receiving those tidings that Hannibal halted at Canusium; and there remained while the decisive blow was struck in the north, which now at length deprived the great Carthaginian of all hope of obtaining that prize for which, during twelve years, he had striven with so much constancy.

Hannibal's object was to fight his way to Hasdrubal, to organise the malcontents of Etruria and Umbria, and to form a new base of operations in the north. The messengers so anxiously looked for were sent, but they never arrived.   Hasdrubal, when he left Placentia, sent off six horsemen to make their way to his brother, with the tidings that he was marching by Ariminum, and with a proposal that they should effect their junction in the plains of Umbria.*   With marvellous good fortune these horsemen made their way through the whole length of Italy, but were all made prisoners near Tarentum, to which place they had wandered in search of Hannibal, who was at the moment in Bruttium.   They were the bearers of a letter from Hasdrubal, not written in cypher but in the common Carthaginian language, which contained the whole plan of his future operations.   The messengers and letter were sent to Nero, who had the writing translated into Latin by one of the African deserters.   That consul took his resolution on the instant.   This was to leave the mass of his army to oppose Hannibal, and to prevent him by all means from moving northward, while he, with 6000 infantry and 1000 cavalry, all picked men, went by forced marches to join his colleague Livius, who was then, according to the report of messengers from that consul, in position behind the Sena River.   He hoped thus by a sudden blow to destroy one brother, and to return to his army in the south before the other should become aware of his absence, and while Hannibal still awaited in Apulia that letter which he was destined never to receive.†

Nero having sent forward horsemen along his intended route bearing orders for the collection at stated spots of all the provisions, carriages and horses which

---

* See Observation 2.   † See Observation 3.

the surrounding districts could furnish, set out on an
enterprise which was to change the destiny of the world.
To prevent the possibility of his design being divulged
to Hannibal, he ordered his selected detachment to prepare for a secret expedition into Lucania ; and it was not
until he had accomplished a considerable distance in his
northward march, that he divulged to his soldiers the
magnitude of the interests which depended on their
speed and courage.   His march was like a triumphal
procession in everything but the pace, for the troops,
worked up to the highest pitch of enthusiasm, would
scarcely halt to take refreshment.   The entire population of the districts through which they passed, lined
the roadside blessing the deliverers of their country.
In seven days the distance, about 270 miles, was accomplished, which could only have been effected by
transporting the soldiers in carts for the greater part of
the way.

Nero's numbers had received a considerable increase
during the march from volunteers, most of them old
soldiers.   Livius was forewarned of his approach, and
Nero entered the camp of his colleague by night, by
which means the arrival of the reinforcement was as
successfully concealed from Hasdrubal as its departure
had been from his brother ; and to prevent suspicion
being excited by an increase in the size of the camp,
the new comers were received in the tents already
standing.

A council of war was held, and though Livius pressed
Nero to allow his men some rest, the latter so urged the
necessity of not losing a single day lest the dreaded

Hannibal should be upon their rear, that it was decided to fight at once.

At daybreak the Roman army formed in order of battle; and Hasdrubal, whose camp was only half a mile distant, accepted the challenge and drew out his troops to engage the consuls. But before attacking, he rode forward to reconnoitre the enemy, and being struck with their apparently increased force, and by other circumstances which appeared suspicious, he led back his men into their camp and sent out scouts to obtain information. Their report, it is said, convinced him that both the consuls were in his front; and believing that some great disaster to Hannibal alone could have set free Nero to oppose himself in the north, he evacuated his camp at nightfall and retreated towards the Metaurus River.*

It is said that Hasdrubal was forsaken by his guides; that in the dark the troops lost their way; that at length after a fatiguing march during the whole of the next day, they arrived on the bank of the Metaurus, but not at the right spot, just as evening closed; that marching up the river to find the fords, they were overtaken by the Roman advanced guard, which attacked their rear and cut off many stragglers; and that Hasdrubal then encamped for the night in the most dangerous position in which an army retreating before an enemy can encamp, that is to say, with an impassable river in his rear, although in other respects the ground offered him a favourable position for fighting. The

* See Observation 4.

effect of a retreat on the spirit of a lively, fickle people like the Gauls, is always depressing; Hasdrubal's Gaulish allies became unmanageable, and in the morning numbers of them were senseless from drink.

At daybreak Hasdrubal formed his troops to meet the attack of the Roman army, which had by that time come up and was advancing against him in order of battle. We have no reliable statement of Hasdrubal's force, but it is certain he was greatly outnumbered by the Romans. Nothing is said of his cavalry. His left wing was covered in front by a rivulet which flowed through a rocky ravine, and which by sweeping round his left flank, secured that also. This being by far the strongest part of his position, he here placed the Gaulish infantry on which he placed little reliance. By thus weakly occupying this part, he was enabled to place his chosen troops at the points where the battle would be decided.* His Ligurian allies he placed in the centre; from them he expected good service; but his best infantry, composed of his veteran Spaniards and some Africans, he placed on the right; and he hoped with these to gain a decisive advantage in that quarter, before the nature of the ground enabled the enemy to come to close quarters with his left wing. His ten elephants he posted in front of the right and centre.

The battle commenced by a general attack of the Roman line from right to left. Livius, who commanded on the left, and Porcius in the centre, met with the

---

* See Observation 5.

most determined resistance and were unable to make the smallest impression. Hasdrubal's elephants, as usual, were equally troublesome to both parties. On the Roman right, meanwhile, Nero, long struggling with the disadvantages of the ground, at last perceived it was impossible to attack the Gauls in his front to any good purpose; but, as they would find the same difficulty in any attempt they might make to attack him, he left a very small force to watch the Gauls, while by a sudden movement he carried the mass of the Roman right wing in rear of the centre and left, and making a rapid circuit, he charged the Spaniards and Africans on their right flank and rear while they were hotly engaged in front. This movement decided the battle. The Spaniards and Ligurians, outnumbered and surrounded, fell where they stood resisting to the last. Hasdrubal, when he saw that the battle was hopelessly lost, spurred his horse into the midst of a Roman cohort, and there found a glorious death.

The loss on both sides is variously stated. Polybius gives that of the vanquished at 10,000, and the Roman loss at 2000 men. Be that as it may, the dreaded army of Hasdrubal was as completely extinct as though it had never existed, and Rome was saved, for Hannibal's single army could not conquer Italy even under such a leader.

Immediately after this great success Nero hastened back to his army in Apulia, carrying with him the ghastly trophy of his victory in the head of Hasdrubal, which, with shocking brutality, he ordered to be thrown down in scorn before the enemy's outposts. This being

carried to Hannibal, revealed to him at the same time
the death of his brother and of all his own most che-
rished hopes.

Rome was almost delirious with joy, and the moral
effect of the battle of the Metaurus, both on the citizens
and their allies, must have been immense. The enmity
of Cisalpine Gaul, the disaffection of Etruria and
Umbria, were no longer to be feared. For almost the
first time during twelve years Rome breathed freely,
and for the first time also during that period the eyes of
her citizens were gladdened with the pomp and splen-
dour of the triumph of a victorious general.

OBSERVATIONS ON THE PRECEDING CHAPTER.

1. Hannibal had, in the course of ten years, taught
the Romans to make war. Had he made such a movement on Rome under the same relative circumstances
during the first years of the contest, it would almost
certainly have produced the only effect he hoped from
it, viz. the raising of the siege of Capua. Being disappointed, his return to Capua was useless: 50,000 Roman
troops still maintained the blockade. Supposing he had
desired to march to Capua, he could not have gone by
the Latin road, for he would have had Fabius and
Fulvius hanging on his rear. And if he returned by the
circuitous route on which he had advanced, Fulvius
could have been at Capua before him, and he would
have found the condition of the garrison worse than that
which his march to Rome was intended to relieve.

The fall of Capua compelled Hannibal to change his
system of warfare. When the Romans became undisputed masters of Campania, the position of that province enabled them to threaten at once Samnium and
Lucania. Hannibal was therefore obliged to concentrate
his force, and to abandon all the small places he held in
those provinces, retaining only the important towns.
His only base now became the southern coast of Italy.

2. Hasdrubal sent off six horsemen in a body to find
Hannibal with a letter, which, if taken, would reveal

his real plans to the enemy. He showed himself wanting in invention. He should have sent off a messenger every day until he received word that one of them had arrived, and each messenger should have had a letter containing a false plan, to mislead, but the real plan should have been entrusted to the brain of the messenger alone. By this means the Romans would have been misled, while Hannibal would have received the information he required to enable him to act.

The catastrophe of the campaign was principally owing to the unskilful arrangements of Hasdrubal in this particular, for Nero would have remained as ignorant as Hannibal of the plans of Hasdrubal if no letter had been found on the messengers. And, on the other hand, if Hannibal had received the information he waited for, he would have instantly attacked Nero; and, judging by what was past, he might have disabled the consul from interfering with his northward march.

3. The march of Nero is one of the finest strategical movements on record. Objections have been made that he ran a great risk of Hannibal discovering his absence and following in his rear. It is true he did so; but Hannibal, marching through a hostile country with the army of Apulia, which Nero had left, hanging on his rear, could not have gone very fast. The distance 270 miles, which, by dint of the assistance of the entire population, Nero accomplished in seven days, would, under the most favourable circumstances, have taken Hannibal fourteen, more probably twenty. Nero's calculations were based on the suddenness of his appearance in the north, and probably on confidence in his

own military genius: he hoped to destroy Hasdrubal by one blow, sudden and decisive, and to return to Apulia in time to oppose Hannibal. War is a game of chances, and a general who risks nothing will gain nothing; his business is to reduce the risks to a minimum. Nero had time on his side, and time is a more valuable ally than any other. He took every possible precaution, particularly as regards secrecy, even keeping his own soldiers ignorant of their destination.*

The march of Nero is as perfect an example as can be afforded of the advantage of interior lines of operation.

The obstacles which existed to the junction of the two brothers were created by the fact that they were operating on exterior lines. The obstacles themselves were:—

No. 1. The numerous armies interposed between them.

No. 2. The want of concert between them from the absence of communication.

No. 1 might have been overcome if No. 2 had been removed, but No. 2 was fatal.†

4. There is something in Hasdrubal's conduct it is difficult to understand. If he was advancing confidently to attack 40,000 men, it does not clearly appear why he so suddenly changed his resolution. It is supposed that it was the knowledge that Nero was in the hostile camp, and the belief that therefore some disaster must have

---

* See page 24, " Theory of War," on the Value of Secrecy.
† See " Theory of War," Lines of Operation, page 77.

happened to his brother. Hasdrubal could only know of the arrival of Roman reinforcements either from the report of spies, or from the results of his own observation. If from spies, they would certainly tell him that the Consul Nero had arrived, but they would also tell him of the very small force by which he was accompanied, which would show that he had left his army to watch Hannibal in the south, and dispel the idea of any great disaster to his brother.

If he learnt the presence of a third Roman general in the hostile camp from observation, from the sounding of trumpets as some say, or otherwise, how could he know that the new arrival was Nero at all? It was much more probable to conclude that it was Varro, who might have been called up with his army from Etruria.

It seems probable enough that Hasdrubal retreated with the design of gaining the Flaminian road, which led from the north side of the Metaurus over the Apennines directly into Umbria, where he expected to meet Hannibal. The advance to the Sena River was therefore a false movement, for the great object was not to beat a single Roman army, but to unite with Hannibal. Having followed Livius to the Sena however, Hasdrubal did not sufficiently weigh the effect of a retreat, both on his own troops and on the malcontents of Etruria and Umbria, who were anxiously watching his progress. In his place probably Hannibal, Turenne, or Condé, would have fought on the Sena, trusting to the prestige which attended a son of Hamilcar.

Compare Hasdrubal's conduct with that of Turenne, when, in command of 16,000 men, he was surprised by the approach of a hostile force of 30,000. Instead of retreating Turenne advanced.*

5. Hasdrubal's method of occupying his position is an example of Maxim 19 (page 151) of the "Theory of War." And the reader is referred to the description of the battle of Ramillies, at page 339 of the same book. He will find that the manœuvre by which Marlborough won the battle is identical with that of Nero, in withdrawing troops from the right wing to reinforce the decisive point on the left. He will also find that Marlborough's movement was made under precisely the same circumstances relative to the enemy, viz. the existence between the opposing wings of the hostile armies at that point of obstacles which prevented either from attacking the other.

6. The victories of Scipio in Spain were in all probability the salvation of Rome. Had he not deprived Hasdrubal of the south coast of Spain, and of the harbours there situated, Hasdrubal with his army would have proceeded to the southern coast of Italy by sea, there to disembark under the protection of Hannibal. The chances of the obstruction of the expedition by a Roman fleet were much fewer than were the chances against the brothers being able to effect a junction when separated by the whole length of Italy, and when six Roman armies were interposed between them.

We know that at a later period, when, owing to the continued successes of Scipio in Spain, the power of Rome relative to Carthage had greatly increased, Han-

* See page 199, "Theory of War," on the Moral Effect of Boldness in War.

nibal effected the much more difficult operation of embarking his whole force in the face of hostile armies at a port in Bruttium, and that he arrived safely at Leptis in Africa.

The unsettled state of Cisalpine Gaul and Etruria had for some time past required the constant presence of a Roman army in each, and the same would still be necessary although Hasdrubal should land in Bruttium. It would have sufficed to send Carthaginian officers of experience to excite the Gauls and Etrurians to rise by the information of Hasdrubal's expedition and to organise their efforts.

CONCLUDING CHAPTER.

THE defeat and death of Hasdrubal obliged Hannibal to remain entirely on the defensive. He retired into Bruttium, and still maintained himself in that province against a host of enemies during four years. Though abandoned entirely to himself, the resources of his great mind supplied everything, and his genius is more to be admired in this decline of his fortunes than during the most brilliant period of his success. Exact details of the operations of these years do not exist, but the fact remains that Hannibal maintained a contest with the numerous forces of Rome in her own territory for four years after the death of Hasdrubal; that such was his personal superiority, that his enemies never dared to engage him in a pitched battle; that when he did evacuate Italy, it was because he was recalled by the Carthaginians to defend them against Scipio; and that he then effected the embarkation of his army in perfect security.

In Spain, Scipio, who in the first year of his command (209 B.C.) had taken New Carthage, and by his policy and personal fascination detached most of the Spaniards from the Carthaginian alliance, had in the second year defeated Hasdrubal at Bæcula. After that victory, he

long and patiently guarded the passes of the Eastern
Pyrenees, to prevent Hasdrubal from entering Gaul;
and on finding that his watchfulness had been in vain,
he sent a part of his own army by sea to Etruria, to aid
in opposing Hasdrubal in Italy. The campaign of the
year 207 B.C. in Spain, was not marked by anything decisive; but in 206 Scipio gained the crowning victory of
Ilinga over Hasdrubal Gisco, which destroyed the last
remnant of the Carthaginian dominion in Spain. He
also succeeded in detaching Massinissa, a Numidian
prince, from Carthage, and even went secretly to Africa
to endeavour to gain over Syphax the Massisilian king,
in which, however, he did not succeed. On his return
to Spain he quelled an insurrection of Spaniards, as
well as a dangerous mutiny in his own army.

Mago, brother to Hannibal, who was the last Carthaginian commander in Spain, perceived that his country's
cause in that peninsula was for the present lost; he
accordingly attempted a diversion in favour of Hannibal,
by landing in Liguria, where he surprised the town of
Genoa early in 205 B.C. His name attracted many
adherents among the Gauls and Ligurians, and his
growing influence obliged the Romans to keep a large
army in the north of Italy to oppose him. Mago
maintained himself there until the year 203; and a few
weeks before the final departure of Hannibal from Italy,
he engaged in an obstinately contested battle with four
Roman legions, in which he received a wound whereof
he died shortly after on his voyage to Africa, to which
country he was recalled to oppose the alarming progress
of Scipio.

Scipio meanwhile after his services in Spain, returned to Rome, was elected consul B.C. 205, and began to prepare to attack the Carthaginians in Africa, as the only means of delivering Italy from the presence of Hannibal. He assembled a powerful fleet and army in Sicily, with which he embarked in the spring of the year 204 B.C. at Lilybæum, and landed without obstruction within a few miles of Carthage. His strength is variously stated, but it would appear that he had three legions, and his numbers therefore amounted probably to 30,000 infantry, and about 2700 cavalry. Forty war galleys in two divisions formed the van, and covered the 400 transports in which the troops were distributed. It is worthy of remark that Scipio made choice of the two legions which had been formed out of the survivors of Cannæ, which had been ever since that battle treated as condemned legions and had been employed in Sicily. He was induced to make this choice partly because those troops having been constantly on active service, were the most expert and experienced soldiers of the republic; but chiefly on account of the moral advantages he expected to derive from their employment. He knew that the men of those legions were keenly sensible of the disgrace with which they had been branded by the stern, though perhaps politic severity of the Roman military code, and that they burned to wipe out the shame of a defeat for which Scipio knew they could not justly be blamed; and the result fully answered his expectations.

Scipio having been joined by Massinissa and a strong body of Numidians, first attempted the siege of Utica, which however the approach of Hasdrubal Gisco and his ally Syphax with a large army of Carthaginians and Numidians obliged him to relinquish. He therefore occupied a strong position near the sea, where, supported and provisioned by his fleet, he determined to pass the winter.

The enemy encamped six miles distant from him. Scipio vainly endeavoured during the winter to gain over Syphax; but the information which he obtained from the messengers who were constantly passing and repassing between him and that prince, of the localities of the hostile camp, enabled him to set it on fire in the night, and having previously stopped up the outlets with his troops, the armies of Hasdrubal and Syphax were either destroyed or dispersed.

Scipio after this success, resumed the siege of Utica, and shortly after defeated another army of 30,000 men which the confederates had collected. After their defeat, Hasdrubal fled to Carthage; Syphax to Numidia.

Scipio now divided his forces, and leaving his fleet to blockade Utica, sent his friend Lælius with Massinissa in pursuit of Syphax with part of his army; while with the remainder he advanced towards Carthage, subduing the surrounding towns and accumulating great plunder.

Syphax having risked a third battle, was defeated, himself made prisoner and his capital taken.

Scipio advanced as far as Tunis, and finding that important place abandoned by its garrison, he established himself there, hoping by his position so close to Car-

thage to terrify that city into submission. The Carthaginians sent messengers to recall Hannibal and Mago
from Italy, and an attempt was made to raise the blockade of Utica by destroying the Roman fleet. But this
attempt failed, and the defeat and capture of Syphax,
news of which was now received, appearing to render
hopeless the further prosecution of the war, the senate
of Carthage sued for and obtained peace from Scipio
on the following humiliating conditions, viz. — 1st. The
evacuation of Italy and Gaul. 2ndly. The cession of
Spain and all the islands between Italy and Africa.
3rdly. The surrender of all their ships of war except
twenty. 4thly. The payment of an immense contribution in corn and money. The treaty was sent to
Rome for ratification, and a truce concluded.

Hannibal landed at Leptis towards the close of the
year. He remained during the winter at Adrumetum.
The Carthaginians, emboldened by his arrival, broke the
truce by detaining some Roman transports which were
driven by a storm into the bay of Carthage; and afterwards attacked the officers sent by Scipio to demand
satisfaction. Hostilities were therefore resumed, and
Hannibal, having united to his own the troops of his
late brother Mago as well as the new African levies,
advanced to the neighbourhood of Zama, a town situated,
according to Polybius, about five days' march to the
south-west of Carthage. He here demanded and obtained a personal interview with Scipio who was there
encamped, but without result, and on the next day the
hostile armies were arrayed against each other for the
last decisive struggle.

Massinissa, a few days before, had brought Scipio a reinforcement of 6000 infantry and 4000 Numidian cavalry. The Roman force may therefore be considered as 30,000 infantry and 6700 cavalry.

The superiority in cavalry, which had always hitherto been in favour of Hannibal, was in this instance reversed; his African cavalry was equal in number to the legionary horse, but it was newly raised, and he had only 2000 Numidians: on the other hand he had eighty elephants, and, it is supposed, about 50,000 infantry.

The Roman heavy infantry was formed as usual in three lines; but the maniples of the second and third lines, instead of covering the intervals of the line in front, were placed one behind another, so that avenues were left between the maniples extending from front to rear. The light troops were placed loosely in the intervals of the first line with orders to attack the elephants, and entice them down the passages to the rear of the Roman army. Massinissa with the Numidian cavalry, was posted on the right flank; Lælius with the legionary horse, on the left.

Hannibal placed his eighty elephants in front of the whole, and formed his infantry in three lines.

The first line consisted of the Ligurians, Gauls, &c., who formed the remnant of Mago's army, to the number of 12,000.

The second line, of the new levies of Africans and native Carthaginians, of nearly the same strength.

The third line, commanded by Hannibal himself, composed of his Italian veterans, numbering about 24,000 men, was kept in reserve at a sufficient distance in rear of the other two lines to allow the fugitives from those lines, if defeated, to escape round the flanks.

The African cavalry was on the right, opposed to Lælius; the Numidians were opposite to Massinissa on the left.

The battle commenced by the advance of the elephants. Of these animals, some terrified by the Roman trumpets which purposely made a great noise, broke off to both flanks and threw Hannibal's cavalry into confusion, which was then charged and easily driven off the field by Massinissa on the one hand, and Lælius on the other.

The remainder of the elephants followed the Roman light troops down the avenues to the rear of the Roman army.

It is said that Scipio having got rid of the elephants, closed the maniples of his first line to the centre so as to leave no intervals, and then ordered it to charge — the second and third lines following slowly in their original formation, protected the flanks of the first.

Hannibal's first line fought with great courage, but the superiority of the Roman arms and discipline prevailed, and being unsupported by the African militia of the second line it was obliged to give way — then these foreigners, believing themselves betrayed by the Carthaginians, fell on their own second line with great fury — and the Romans charging at the same time, Hannibal's second line was overthrown.

But Scipio had now to encounter a more severe struggle. Hannibal still had a body of 24,000 infantry which had not been engaged; and that infantry con-

sisted of the Italian veterans, Hannibal's old guard,
whose habits of victory and unlimited confidence in
their commander would have made them formidable to
double their number of enemies.   Scipio's infantry,
originally 30,000, had suffered considerable loss, and
was, to a certain extent, disordered by the struggle.
The Roman commander might well look anxiously for
some signs of his cavalry, which carried away by the
ardour of pursuit, had followed the enemy too far from
the field.   Hannibal perceiving all the advantage of his
position, advanced to attack the Roman infantry, hoping
to defeat it before the cavalry should return.   Scipio
had barely time to prolong his first line, which consisted
of only 9600 men, to both flanks, by calling up maniples
from the second and third lines — in order to oppose an
equal front to Hannibal's reserve which consisted of
24,000 men, drawn up in the same order as the
Romans, in ten ranks.   The struggle was obstinate; it
would in all probability have terminated in favour of
Hannibal, but fortune had deserted him for a younger
favourite, and Lælius and Massinissa with the Roman
cavalry returned just at the right moment to charge the
Carthaginians in rear, while they were engaged in front.
Surrounded and overpowered, that veteran infantry,
before which the Roman standards had so often re-
ceded, yet maintained its high reputation; most of
them were cut down where they stood, and few escaped
from the field, for the country was level and the Roman
and Numidian horse were active in pursuit.

As soon as Hannibal saw that the battle was hopelessly lost, knowing that now his country would have

greater need of him than ever, he displayed a higher
fortitude than his brother Hasdrubal, and escaped off
the field to Adrumetum.

With the battle of Zama terminated all attempt at
resistance to the power of Rome. Scipio dictated the
following conditions on which alone he would grant
them peace; viz. that the Carthaginians were to make
amends for the injuries done to the Romans during the
truce ; to give up all their ships of war except ten, and
all their elephants; to restore all Roman prisoners and
deserters; to engage in no war out of Africa; and to
engage in none in Africa without the consent of Rome;
to restore to Massinissa the kingdom of which he had
been deprived; to feed the Roman army for three
months; to pay a contribution of 200 Euboic talents
a year for fifty years; and to give 100 hostages
between the ages of 14 and 30, to be selected by the
Roman general.

These hard terms were perforce accepted by the
Carthaginians; and their fulfilment left that unfortu-
nate people no real power to resist the injustice and
aggression of Rome, which at length resulted in the
Third Punic War, and in the final destruction of their
city and dominion.

Hannibal lived nineteen years after the battle of
Zama. He devoted himself to the service and improvement of his countrymen; but his exposure and recti-
fication of the gross abuses of the public service,
raised up against him powerful enemies who drove him
into exile in the year B.C. 196. He then repaired to
the court of Antiochus, king of Syria, who was at that

time engaged in a war against Rome. But that monarch had not the wisdom to follow the advice Hannibal gave him, and his defeat at Magnesia resulted in a treaty of peace, one of the terms of which was the delivery of the illustrious refugee into the hands of his most bitter enemies.

Hannibal, on being warned of the design against him, became again a wanderer. He repaired to the court of Prusias, King of Bithynia; but Rome could not be easy so long as her great enemy lived. And Hannibal eventually, it is said, died by his own act in the sixty-fourth year of his age, in consequence of a demand made upon Prusias by the Romans for his delivery to them, which that monarch had neither the power nor the spirit to resist.

OBSERVATIONS.

The foregoing description of the battle of Zama differs from all existing accounts in one particular. All the descriptions of that battle state, that after having defeated Hannibal's two first lines, Scipio drew off his troops and formed them again before venturing to attack the formidable body of infantry in his front, which was nearly equal in number to his own and perfectly fresh ; that having paused a considerable time to enable his men to effect their formation and to recover breath, he at length gave the signal to advance against Hannibal, who during all this period passively awaited his attack; and that while the infantry was engaged in an equal contest, the cavalry of Scipio fortunately returned in the nick of time to decide the battle in his favour.

On this it may be remarked that this account would make out both Hannibal and Scipio to be utter incapables.

Scipio was quite right in pausing, according to that account, to form his men and to give them breath for a new attack, if Hannibal was so accommodating as to allow him. But if the initiative really rested with Scipio, it was the height of rashness to attack 24,000 veterans in an equal field, when he was expecting the return of his cavalry which would have turned the scale decisively in his favour. Therefore if Scipio took the initiative, it may be regarded as certain that he was anxiously straining his eyes to catch sight of his cavalry, and when he did catch sight of them *then* and not till then did he give the signal for attack.

But a different version of the battle has been given in these pages, because, on the other hand, it is utterly incredible that Hannibal should have allowed Scipio to take the initiative. The reasons given by the historians for Hannibal's formation of his reserve so far in rear of the two first lines, are not only that the fugitives from the two first lines, if defeated, should have plenty of room to save themselves round the flanks of the reserve without running in upon and disordering it, but that the victorious Romans who would be pressing on in pursuit, disordered by the shock and the struggle, might then be assailed while in confusion by this fresh body of troops. And it must have been with this design that Hannibal's third line was made equal in strength to the other two lines together.

Can it be believed then that Hannibal, knowing the Roman cavalry was absent but that it might be expected soon to return, would fail to avail himself of the golden opportunity, and should wait tamely with his men like sheep to be slaughtered in a pen until the butchers had sharpened their knives?

The conduct of Lælius and Massinissa as cavalry commanders, is only one instance out of many of the necessity of coolness in the commander, and perfect discipline among the men. See " Theory of War," page 240.

It is remarkable that the manœuvre which turned the battle of Zama against him, was an exact counterpart of the one which decided the battle of Cannæ in Hannibal's favour.

Hannibal's genius as a general has hardly ever been equalled, never certainly surpassed.

His resolution to undertake the conquest of Italy with 20,000 infantry and 6000 cavalry, without any certain base of operations, manifests that confidence in himself which—although when ill-founded it is the sure mark of incapacity—when well-founded, is the highest proof of inspiration, and without which in war nothing great can be achieved.

His organisation of Cisalpine Gaul into a secure base of operations, and of its fickle inhabitants into allies whose fidelity and devotion to him never swerved under the most adverse fortune, present that wonderful combination of personal fascination and knowledge of human nature which enabled him to influence his fellow-men in so remarkable a degree; and which, when joined to his complete mastery over all the mere physical agents in war, rendered him irresistible.

The Trebbia, Cannæ, and Thrasymene, were brilliant victories, but it is not by their light that the genius of this great man is most clearly revealed. The generals there opposed to him, though brave soldiers and in some respects able men, were ignorant of the art of war. But after Cannæ the Romans adopted a system of operations which was in general as skilfully executed as wisely conceived. Fabius, Marcellus, Fulvius, Gracchus,

Nero, all great men and good generals, surrounded him with their armies; harassed his outposts and foraging parties; cut off his supplies whenever they could; dogged him in all his marches; yet were never able to prevent him from coming and going at his pleasure and never once gained an important advantage over him personally. Even after the death of Hasdrubal, his numerous enemies, like dogs baiting a bear, only barked and snapped without daring to encounter his hug. When he at length quitted Italy his embarkation was undisturbed; and it is very doubtful if he would have been forced to quit that country at all had he not been recalled by Carthage. Even Scipio seems to have been unwilling to encounter Hannibal in Italy.

On more than one occasion, as has been already remarked, Hannibal violated the arbitrary rules of war by placing himself in situations, which to men of less transcendant ability would have been ruin. But he measured correctly the capacity of his adversaries and his own, and that which in another would have been rashness, was in him only the fruit of the most deliberate and just calculation.

In this respect he resembles Alexander and indeed all great generals. Alexander commenced the conquest of Asia Minor with a force little superior to that with which Hannibal descended from the Alps. He manifested the same ability in creating a base of operations and acquiring allies, or rather (in his case) subjects, whom his policy retained faithful to him. As instances of his contempt of mere rules as such, Alexander fought the battle of Issus with a narrow pass behind him and the army of Darius interposed between him and his natural line of retreat.

He fought the battle of Arbela, having the Tigris, the Euphrates, and the desert in his rear, in the heart of an enemy's country, and having no depôt nearer than Tyre.

Napoleon says, in remarking on the campaigns of Cæsar : " Cæsar's principles were the same as those of Alexander and Hannibal — to keep his forces united; not to be vulnerable in more places than absolutely necessary; to throw himself rapidly on important points; to employ largely moral means, viz. the reputation of his arms, the fear which he inspired, and politic measures calculated to preserve the attachment of the allies and the submission of his conquered provinces."

These great men, confident in their own powers, set at nought the rules of war whenever more was to be gained by neglecting than by observing them, and they were justified by success. But woe to that general who, overestimating his own abilities, seeks to imitate the great masters in this particular ; he will meet only with failure and disgrace.

NOTE. — The reader is referred to "Theory of War," Chap. vi., on Moral Agents in War. He will there find an enumeration of qualities required in a general, which were all possessed by Hannibal in the highest degree, and the whole of his military career is moreover a striking illustration of all the further remarks contained in that chapter.

THE END.

REFERENCES TO *THE THEORY OF WAR.*

p. 24 Secrecy

Secrecy is a main condition of success in the execution of a military plan. The greatest captains have made a practice of keeping their design strictly to themselves until the very moment of execution. Marlborough was conspicuous for his reserve in this respect and as examples of secrecy, as well as of his genius in the employment of moral as distinguished from physical agents, his great march to the Danube in 1704, previous to Blenheim, and the manoeuvres by which he deceived Villars and forced the formidable lines constructed by that marshal to cover the French frontier in 1711, are recommended to the careful attention of the student. Both of the above operations are models of strategy, manifesting in the highest degree all the qualities of a great captain.

At the present time, when every camp swarms with "Special Correspondents," shows particular business it is to worm out the plans of the general to furnish pabulum for the insatiable maw of curiosity at home, secrecy is more than ever necessary.

p. 59–61

Organisation and discipline.

Are the troops opposed to you veterans or raw levies? Are they well or ill officered? Are they of one race, o composed of men of different races fighting for a dominant people whom they detest? Can they manoeuvre with rapidity and precision? With a

veteran army opposed to young troops; with an army well officered opposed to one ill officered; with an army of one race and
feeling opposed to one of different races as above; with an army
which manoeuvres well and quickly opposed to one which can do
neither; act boldly, endeavour to force your enemy to a general
action,which may be decisive, as soon as possible.

Reverse the conditions, and it is your interest to avoid a decisive battle; to gain time to discipline and drill your men' to
engage in partial contests where the chances are very great in
your favour, to give your soldiers confidence. If forced to fight, let
it be in a position naturally strong, and increase its strength in
every possible way artificially; and above all take care that your
line of retreat is easy and open, and have your plan of retreat
perfectly matured in your own mind.

The spirit of the soldiers, arising from former defeats or vic-
tories.

Napoleon understood probably better than any modern commander how to avail himself of the enthusiasm with which his
victories inspired his solders, as well as of the discouragement
they occasioned to his enemies. A fine example of this is afforded
by his resolution to draw out his forces into the plain at Arcola to
attack the Austrian army on the third day, after the previous tow
days' hard fighting. Napoleon judged that the spirit of the
Austrians must have been seriously depressed by their continued repulse during these two first days by an army of only half
their numbers; and he was induced by that consideration, combined with that of the actual physical loss sustained by his enemies, to adopt the bold and apparently hazardous resolution of
attacking them in the open.

Rapidity and Marching

It may here merely be remarked that one army may be moving on "interior lines" with respect to another solely by reason of its moving more quickly, although every other element, such as distance and obstacles, may be in favour of that other.

The character and skill of the commander.

The following remarks of Napoleon will illustrate this better than the most elaborate treatise:—

"The commander-in-chief is the head he is everything to an army. It was not the Roman army which conquered Gaul, but Caesar. It was not the Carthaginian army which made Rome tremble at her gates, but Hannibal. It was not the Macedonian army which marched to the Indus, but Alexander. It was not the Prussian army which defended Prussia for seven years against the three most powerful states of Europe, but Frederick."

p. 77 Lines of Operation

The principle which particularly applies to them, and must never be violated, is Principle 3, which indicates that your line or lines of operation must be such that the fractions of your army moving upon them shall be more quickly unitable at any decisive point than the fractions of the enemy. Provided these conditions can be fulfilled, lines may be single, double, or multiplied, without violating the rules of war. But as a general rule lines of operation should be as few in number as possible.

p. 151 Maxim 19.

Occupy your position in such a manner that you can defend a part of it with a smaller force than that which the enemy can bring against it, so that the greater part of your force may be available to assail the weaker of the enemy. e.g. If two armies A and B, of 20,000 men each, occupy lines of equal length; but A, by reason of the ground being naturally stronger on the right half of his line, or by reason of entrenchments, is able to occupy that half effectively with only 5000 men, while the force of B is equally disseminated, then (to use a technical term) the 5000 of A *contain* 10,000 of B; while A has 15,000 wherewith to over-whelm the opposing 10,000 of B.

p. 199 Moral Effect of Boldness

Several examples of the great moral effect of a bold course in averting disaster are drawn from the campaigns of Turenne; one is given here, having a direct reference to this subject; the rest illustrate equally other general rules, and will be found else-where.

In 1653, Turenne commanded the French army of 16,000 men, of which 10, 000 were cavalry. A Spanish army of 30,000 men, under the Archduke of Condé, invaded Picardy, and threat-ened to march on Paris where there was great consternation. Opinions were divided as to the best course to pursue. Some pro-posed to employ 5000 of the infantry to garrison the places which were on the Archduke's line of operations on Paris, and with the remainder to harass the enemy's line of march, to cut off his stragglers, intercept his convoys, &c.

Others rejected the idea of dividing the army, and proposed that it should take post behind the Oise to defend the passage of that rive' and when forced, that it should fall back on Paris where it could be joined by the succours which delay would bring from the provinces.

Turenne favoured neither scheme. It was impossible to prevent the passage of such a river as the Oise; yet, when the enemy should succeed in forcing it, he as well as the Parisians would magnify the success, and its influence on the *morale* of the army would be most depressing.

The plan which he adopted was to march always on a parallel line with the enemy at the distance of twelve or fourteen miles; to wage a warfare of marches and manoeuvres. His soldiers would thus have no reason to believe themselves inferior to the enemy, and time would bring reinforcements which might enable him to assume the offensive. The conception was on the whole skillfully executed.

On the 13th of August, however, the army of Turenne was surprised when near Mont St. Quentin by the intelligence of the approach of the Spanish army.

The alarm was great; Turenne drew up his force in order of battle; but his left was so badly posted, being commanded on all sides by heights which the superiority of the enemy would enable him to occupy, that to remain in his position was certain defeat. Meanwhile the enemy was approaching. The country which separated the hostile armies being mountainous, Turenne resolved—instead of retreating as an ordinary general might have done—to advance, in the certainty of finding a better position than that which he was about to quit. Accordingly he had not marched more than two miles and a half when he found what he sought. His left rested on an almost inaccessible height, and his front was covered by a stream which flows into the Somme at Peronne. At three in the afternoon the Spanish army presented itself. Condé wished to attack Turenne at once; but the Archduke said his troops were fatigued and they must first have a night's rest. The French profited by the delay to intrench themselves; and next day the Spanish generals though their position too strong. After remaining before it three days the Spanish army decamped.

p. 240

In a successful charge, cavalry are very apt to be tempted to pursue too far. A cavalry commander should always bear in mind the fate of Rupert at Naseby, and of John de Vert at Nordlingen, and keep his squadrons well in hand. If the routed squadrons of the enemy are pursued off the field of battle, as is frequently the case, both sides are in the same relative position as before; an equal number of squadrons are absent; that is all; whereas, if the victorious squadrons remained on the field, they might influence decisively the other events of the day.

Hannibal owed nearly all his victories to the discipline of his cavalry and excellence of its commanders, who, after driving the hostile cavalry off the field, invariably returned to assist in the destruction of the hostile infantry.

Alexander of Macedon, 10, 11, 14, 16, 47, 194

Antiochus, 189

Appian road, 115

Appius Claudius, 135, 140, 150

Archimedes, 134

Atillius, 31, 37, 75, 98

Balearic slingers, 41

Beneventum, battle of, 137, 138

Campania, Carthaginian operations in, 129–131

Cannae, battle of, 85, 88–97, 110, 193

Capua, defeat of, 151–156

Carthage, sues for peace, 185, 189

Carthaginian fleet, 108, 111, 136

Caudine Forks, skirmish at, 139

cavalry, African, 187; Gaulish, 37, 59, 92; Numidian, 30, 37, 40, 50, 60, 61, 87, 90, 92, 94, 164, 187; Roman, 93, 94, 151

Centenius, M., 139, 141

Cumae, skirmish at, 118

Crispinius, 159, 162, 164, 165, 167

elephants, 31, 34, 41, 173, 186, 187

Emilius, M., 85, 89, 93, 94, 96, 135, 145

Fabius, 62–74, 82, 83, 114, 117–120, 125–129, 131–133, 135, 144, 145, 154, 158–161, 163, 175, 193

Flaminius, 55–61, 68, 75, 77–80, 109, 164

Fulvius, 135, 137, 140, 145, 150, 153, 157–160, 163, 167, 175, 193

Geronium, skirmishes around, 70–74

guerilla warfare, 115

Gracchus, Tiberius Junius, 114, 117, 119, 120, 124, 125, 129–135, 137, 139, 141, 142, 144-147, 150, 154, 164, 193

Hamilcar, 24, 25, 165, 178

Hannibal, oath of enmity, 24, crosses the Alps, 31–35; crosses Arno River, 58, advance on Rome, 63; escapes from Campania, 66–69; captures magazine at Cannae, 87; use of cavalry at Cannae, 101; forbids ransoms, 110; march on Rome, 153, 154; honors Marcellus, 164, 165; recalled to Carthage, 181, 185; exiled, 189; death, 190

Hanno, 27, 36, 111,112, 113, 129–131, 134, 136, 137, 145, 147, 158

Hasdrubal, 25, 26, 36, 92, 95, 113, 143, 149, 156, 159, 162, 165, 167, 167, 169, 171–173, 176–182, 184, 189

Herdonea, battle of, 141

Hieronymus, 131

Himilcar, 120

infantry, African, 41, 49, 59, 92, 95, 173; Gaulish, 41, 60, 61, 92, 186; Ligurian, 172, 173, 186; Roman, 42, 89, 92, 95, 151, 152, 188; Spanish, 41, 49, 59, 68, 92, 173

Junius, M., 107, 111, 112, 124, 136

Laelius, 184, 186–188, 192

Levinius, 159

Mago, 40, 42, 111, 141, 182, 185

Maharbal, 92, 96, 102, 106

Manlius, 31, 36, 37

Marcellus, 85, 105, 108, 109, 111,
112, 117-120, 122–125, 128, 131,
132, 142, 144, 156, 157, 159–162,
164, 165, 193; action against,
160, 161

Marcus Furius, 108

Marcus Livius, 166, 167, 170, 172,
178

Marcus Valerius, 121, 132, 157, 159

Massinissa, 182-184, 186–189, 192

Metaurus, battle of, 170–174

Minucius, 62, 65, 70–74, 84, 96

Nero,Claudius, 135, 137, 142, 150,
156, 163, 166, 168–171, 173,
176–179, 194

Nola, assault on, 119, 120

Philip of Macedon, 116, 121, 132,
156, 159

Porcius, L., 162, 167

Postumius, L., 86, 112, 114

Quintus Fabius Maximus, 63

Roman fleet, 111, 121, 138, 142,
159

Saguntum, siege of, 26

Sicily, Roman control of, 158

Scipio, Publius, 28, 30, 35–40, 42,
45, 48-50, 54, 76, 113, 120, 132,
156

Scipio, Gnaeus Calvus, 31, 113,
120, 132, 156

Scipio Africanus, 162, 179,
181–189, 191, 192, 194

Sempronius, 35, 39–42, 50, 54, 57,
76

Sempronius Gracchus, 107

Servilius, 55, 57, 74, 77–79, 81, 96,
98

Spain, war in, 24–27, 113, 120, 121,
132, 143, 156, 162, 181, 182

Syphax, 134, 182, 184, 185

Syracuse, siege of, 134, 142, 150,
151

Tarentum, capture of, 134–136; loss
of, 161

Thrasymene, battle of, 20, 59–62

Ticinus, battle of, 37

Trebbia, battle of, 14, 40–42, 50, 51,
69

Utica, siege of, 183

Varro, 85, 88-91, 93, 96, 101, 108,
109, 122, 123, 135, 162, 167, 178

Zama, battle of, 49, 185–189, 191,
193